ADVANCE PRAISE FOR *BLINDSPOT*

Campion's narrative voice assumes the role of your most cherished confidante, your guide to the elusive world of the nondual perspective. "Where did the hours go?" you may well ask yourself, as the dawn breaks after a sleepless night. Such is the compelling draw of this remarkable book. —**Jerry Katz**, founder and host, Nonduality.com

This is a wonderful book, brilliantly, wittily, and lucidly reasoned. It was compelling to me from beginning to end. —**Red Hawk** (aka: Robert Moore, PhD), author of *Self-Remembering, Self-Observation, Return to the Mother,* and *The Way of the Wise Woman.*

Blindspot exposes the unseen distinctions that exist among the ways that people seek the Big Answers to the questions posed by life, the universe, and everything. Campion strips away our blinders with a playful humor. —**Zaya and Maurizio Benazzo**, filmmakers and founders: Science and Nonduality (SAND) global community.

A provocative read for those interested in deepening their own understanding of the important questions in life. —**Mariana Caplan, PhD,** psychotherapist; author: *Halfway Up the Mountain: The Error of Premature Claims to Enlightenment, Yoga & Psyche,* and *Transformation and Joy and Eyes Wide Open.*

Moss Campion invades the high court of spirituality with the wit of a jester, the linguistic skill of a poet, and the wisdom of one who has suffered the "naked, unutterable freefall of realization." I found his approach refreshing, authentic, and containing the one crucial ingredient that goes missing from the vast majority of spiritual literature: playfulness.

Blindspot is a seduction into a private unraveling and a personal undoing that feels kind, welcome, and optimistic. —**Rick Lewis**, motivational speaker; author: *The Perfection of Nothing,* and *7 Rules You Were Born to Break*; and founder of PivottothePodium.com

BLIND SPOT

THROUGH THE WORMHOLE OF SCIENCE AND RELIGION

MOSS CAMPION

HOHM PRESS
CHINO VALLEY, ARIZONA

Cover Design: Hohm Press

Interior Design and Layout: Kubera Book Design, Becky Fulker

Library of Congress Control Number: 2024931609

ISBN: 978-1-942493-94-5

Ebook: 978-1-942493-95-2

Hohm Press
P.O. Box 4410
Chino Valley, AZ 86323
800-381-2700
http://www.hohmpress.com

This book was printed in the U.S.A. on recycled, acid-free paper using soy ink.

CONTENTS

Deep down the consciousness of humanity is one. And if we don't see this it's because we are blinding ourselves to it.

—David Bohm, physicist

The Kingdom is spread out upon the earth
And people do not see it.

—Jesus of Nazareth

INTRODUCTION

This book is a product of frustration. There, you've been warned.

After years of hearing the stunning insights articulated by bright, aware, inquisitive people who were often at the forefront of their respective fields of endeavor, I became stimulated, yet also baffled. Yes, the discoveries being made by these folks in the arts, sciences, religion and philosophy were marvelous and inspiring, and yet… something was almost always missing.

This book addresses that "something."

These pages are aimed at an audience comprised of those same bright folks—no doubt you—who might never have been exposed to an entirely "other" perspective from which to view their investigations into life, the universe, and everything. Or who might have been exposed to it, yet had drawn back from it, as if it were too hot to touch. As if it was some kind of "third rail" of existence.

To say that I am hardly the first person to have ever expressed this perspective would be a gross understatement. Indeed, it has been talked about for millennia all over the world. Yet this paradigm has always seemed to exist in a kind of parallel universe from the one familiar to most people, no matter how well informed they might be. And so it has remained in a kind of blind spot for them. As someone once remarked, "…and people do not see it."*

I have dubbed this lacuna "Blindspot," and this book is an attempt to shine some light into it. The Blindspot exists in a kind of gap that prevails between the ideas and worldviews being lived out by folks everywhere and an even deeper insight that is afforded by the other perspective addressed here. Although I am emphatically not out to

---

* This scriptural passage is usually rendered as "men do not see it," but I have adopted a more inclusive translation in order to spread the pain equally.

convert anyone to my way of thinking, I do hope that this book helps to bridge this gap and bring its two sides closer together. To expose the blind spot and thus reveal the gap for what it really is.

Ah, that's better. Already I feel a bit less frustrated.

1.

GOOD GAWD

God exists. God does not exist. God may or may not exist, and He or She may or may not match Christian, Islamic, or whatever conceptions about His or Her nature—but there is no way to either prove or disprove any of the claims made about Him, Her, or It by any rational argument. Although God knows [sic] many have tried.

So go the unending debates, raging in both popular and academic circles these days, along with all the tributary arguments about the meaning of life (or lack thereof), the nature of the afterlife (or lack thereof), and the existence of free will (or lack thereof). Debates waged not only by religious believers of all stripes, but also by the growing number of people who claim to be not religious but "spiritual," instead. Not to mention the folks who call themselves "secular humanists." Or anyone, for that matter, who has looked around in spare moments and wondered, "What the hell is going on here?"

My intention is to strike a resolving chord to this dissonance by making the claim that God—otherwise known as Truth—*does* exist and can make itself known. When I use the T-word, whether capitalized or not, I am speaking of the same ideal pursued by most genuine scientists and valued by most honest laypeople. Yet we humans actively avoid its possible discovery in all our various discourses, right down to the most intimately personal ones we carry on within ourselves, every moment. For there exists an entirely other perspective that's almost never considered in all these debates; it remains hidden in a kind of blind spot to our view. Yet if that overlooked other possibility were seen, it would become obvious that when most people speak about God or Truth or the Divine, they aren't really talking about anything divine or godly at all, whether they're for Him, against Her, or undecided. They all share an almost universal unseeingness about what the entire spiritual enterprise (read: life) is actually about—its rules, codes, even its final aim. The psycho-historico-neurological reasons for this blind spot may be understandable. Yet its costs to the individual, to humanity in general, to the planet as a whole, are high, indeed. In a word: confusion. In another word: suffering.

And yet this not-seeing occurs with respect to something that's actually widely known. It's been reported about, sung about and studied for millennia—yet all in what amounts to a kind of parallel universe to the common one, from which it remains unregarded. Yet strangely it's also something that is in plain view, closer to us than our own noses.

Or at least that's *my* view, so perhaps I can't get away without declaring my "credentials"—even though mine might not fit the usual academic or titled senses you might expect with a pop-philosophical book such as this. The (relative) truth of the matter is that I possess no such credentials. In a book such as this the test of credential must reside in the words themselves, or it is irrelevant. And the very fact that I have written this book and you are reading it—at least so far—constitutes its own stamp of legitimacy.

If this seems like circular reasoning, it's nothing more than a reflection of the same charming circularity that dogs the entire subject under discussion in these pages. Both the particular perspective on Truth offered here and the creds of those who communicate it are blazingly obvious and self-validating within the system it arises out of, and this has nothing to do with anybody's academic degrees, media platform, or scriptural authority. The constant refrain heard throughout this particular universe is, *Don't take my word for anything; look for yourself.*

To those readers outside the contemplative spiritual subculture—which is (*hello, there!*) the audience for which I've written this screed—I can only say that from this perspective it can be seen without doubt that the avoided truth under question, once revealed, could instantly resolve (though not solve) the thorniest questions facing humanity, from the broadest philosophical ones to the most narrowly private; from the most abstract theoretical ones to the most everyday practical ones. An outrageous claim, to be sure, but as someone once said, the truth does set you free. Although only when it's realized on its own terms. And that's the seemingly circular—although when seen, not actually circular—catch.

That catch is a bitch, for the truth is a minefield for the mind. The aforementioned blind spot rears its (invisible) head over and over, in all times and at all places. It seems to be the first tripwire that most minds are likely to graze, when tiptoeing through the hazards buried in this field. And despite my terrible habit of abusing my metaphors, I ask that you lend me some trust on this rhetorical journey. For the goblin hidden in the blind spot can become self-evident to anybody who *does* look for him- or herself...in the right direction.

So: onward to the Blindspot, or at least some preliminaries. I think it's fair to say there are two primary approaches to, or attitudes toward, spirituality that people generally take today: 1) the following of some religion (any of them), or 2) the identifying with one of those groups born of reactive responses to religion. These latter folks might see themselves as atheists, agnostics, skeptics or just plain secular humanists. Many of them hold the worldview of science in the highest esteem, as their lodestar for what they would call truth. And yes, there are also many who would identify themselves as religious scientists or skeptical believers or some other hybrid combination of the two broad categories. But in any case, every one of these identifications, whether from the religious camp or the non-religious camp, share the same side of a certain gap: they share the same Blindspot.

This book is an introduction to the other side of the gap.

All those interfaith dialogues going on today in public forums everywhere? From this neglected side of the gap, they look like so much twaddle. Well-meaning, perhaps, but essentially meaningless. The wordy mind, chasing its own ever-alluring tail. Ditto for all those science-vs.-religion powwows and those so-called "religious freedom" debates. But as I've said, there exists an entirely different option available to anybody with an interest in truth, even if they call it nothing more than peace or happiness. It lies on the other side of the gap, hidden in the Blindspot; it is precisely in the heart of this vacancy that God (by whatever name) can be most directly accessed. The possibility unnoticed here carries real consequences, and we overlook it at our peril, both personal and collective.

Sure, more and more people in the developed world identify themselves as "spiritual, but not religious"; and this distinction does hint at the other possibility to which I refer. It does hint at the Blindspot. Yet exactly what this means—spiritual vs. religious (or either one vs. humanistic) remains hazy, even among the adherents themselves. It's also usually left unclear as to how this spiritual thing might be at all preferable to the religious thing, if the goal is supposed to have any relevance to truth (which, remember, does in fact exist).

All the more reason for someone like me—who has spent a lifetime in the trenches—to write this book. I mean, how do they all fit together, if they do—all those claims and counterclaims about spirituality, religion and secularism that you might encounter out there? All those testimonies and memoirs, near-death accounts and post-stroke accounts, scientific treatises and channeled transcriptions... How might the poor seeker, or the merely curious, make any sense of this torrent of chatter?

Welcome to my little gauntlet.

I am not just picking at abstract, remote intellectual straws here. It is said that every person without exception is, at heart, a philosopher—for they know that they will die. And this brings a certain hardball urgency to the consideration of truth, not least because we live in a time when not only do we know that we will die, personally, but we suspect that much of planetary life could well be taken out along with us. So, while human beings have always been infected with the philosophical virus called "seeking," current circumstances have made us more culturally self-aware of that fact.

The seeking bug is usually only understood as the pursuit of happiness. And even the most self-identified unspiritual of individuals do spend their lives under its thrall. But when awareness of the seeking impulse clarifies, it starts to disclose its essential nature—an impulse toward peace or wholeness or fulfillment or completion. Sooner or later, however, it becomes apparent that this impulse cannot be satisfied in the usual ways that people find satisfaction, no matter how hard they try. And then the virus begins to earn its metaphors. It starts to feel like "an itch they cannot scratch" (*Blade Runner*) or a "splinter in the mind" (*The Matrix*)—and after that the person is never the same. They then officially become a *spiritual* seeker. Beyond mere viruses, the vampire analogy has sometimes been used in this context. A person thus bitten becomes irreparably altered and inconsolable, stalking the world for relief from his isolation.* One contemporary spiritual teacher describes such a person as afflicted with "divine discontent."

This is not something that most postmodern folks would want to advertise in public. Yet even those cultural pacesetters today courageous enough to admit their own versions of this hunger, often unwittingly betray the presence of the Blindspot. For example, one recent self-professed agnostic writer has coined the term "spiritual envy" in a poignant attempt to describe this essential yearning—his own earnest wish that he could believe in the higher verities most others seem to have no problem with. Similarly, another well-known literary figure confesses to not believing in God anymore, but "missing Him" all the same. And with this sentiment he echoes yet another writer, who in escaping from her evangelical Christian past, plaintively wonders whether she will ever be able to recapture those "selfless feelings" she

---

* The bloodsucking part is conveniently left out of this image.

had in her old church community, now that she has found herself within the orbits of "secular minds and realms."

Such is the nature of the "God-shaped hole" spoken of by Blaise Pascal in the 17th century, which he said existed "in the heart of every man." It's a spiritual vacuum that virtually cries out for filling with something, *anything*—even though what usually ends up in that role is simply not equipped for the job. For most, due to the Blindspot, the hole gets assaulted with the simulacra of imagination and thus does not get filled at all. It remains gaping.

What remains is that deep viral yearning for something real, something meaningful, even if it doesn't fit any prevailing definition of religious. It's a yearning for a kind of contextual ground that seems to arise unbidden during the course of most people's lives—folks you would never suspect, people who generally keep their tiny demons under wraps, at least while in polite company. Are they perhaps sensing the presence of some itchy possibility that's there, just out of sight, but that they can't quite put their finger on?

Not known for being polite, Walt Whitman described this inchoate itch with a great wonder:

> There is that in me—I do not know what it is—but it is in me.
> ...It is without name—it is a word unsaid,
> It is not in any dictionary, utterance, symbol.
> ...Do you see O my brothers and sisters?
> It is not chaos or death—it is form, union, plan—it is
> eternal life—it is happiness.[1]

Still others are broadsided in life—or by near-death collisions—by actual experiences that can only be called mystical, in which they confront the direct, shattering perception of their own radiant unity with the universe, or some such description. Such folks then proceed to either suppress the feelings triggered by these experiences (for fear of being labelled crazy by their peers), or to pursue furtive lifelong searches for answers within the usual cultural constraints (which keep them blind to the treasures awaiting outside those boundaries). Neither of these strategies satisfy the nagging questions that such powerful experiences raise. And since for many people, spontaneous experiences of this kind occur in childhood, they often end up becoming nothing more than dim memories in a life whose spiritual process has stalled out.

The situation in academia isn't much better. A famous philosophic scholar was recently profiled in a national magazine that hailed his lifelong search to find the ultimate source of human morality. Yet although he was the recipient of many honors and awards, the said scholar (by his own admission) had still not achieved his goal. All he had done was to split the cognitive hairs of his search into finer and finer pieces, while discovering that every fine hair only gives rise to still finer hairs, ad infinitum. Brilliantly exposed, perhaps, but ultimately unsatisfying; the question of morality unanswered. Which is something that anyone familiar with the alternative way described in this book could have told him thousands of years ago. For to split hairs is simply the nature of mind; it's just what minds are designed to do: to split hairs, but never to come to a stop.

The quest in the realm of science shares many of these same foibles, and we shall itemize them in detail later. Yet however people may end up confronting the Truth question in their lives, most will act out their yearnings by either returning to the religious forms of their upbringing or transferring their zeal over to some other type of recognized religion. Either that or, in rejecting all those branded forms, by finally announcing themselves as atheists or agnostics or humanists or Druids or whatever other ethico-philosophical hybrid might appeal to them. The hint of any mysterious third option—the possibility that would collapse any gap, expose any blind spot, and open to them the abyss of truth—will simply not be apparent to them. It won't appear on the spiritual menu in most places.

And if I didn't know what I know about knowing, this state of affairs would drive me nuts. Instead, it's driven me to write a book, which might be even nuttier.

The scenario I portray would be much bleaker, however, were it not for the insights unfolding today at the cutting edges of science and philosophy, where numerous folks are chipping away at the Blindspot described here. It's no secret in many quarters today that the discoveries of the past hundred years in physics and biology are displaying some remarkable convergences with the testimonies of spiritual sages from ages past. Yet the precise nature of these convergences is often misunderstood by both the public and the scientists themselves. Such confusions constitute a hornet's nest that any wise person would avoid addressing at all costs; but, as we shall see, this author may not merit that description.

The job is complicated by the fact that although those scientists and philosophers working at the boundaries of their fields are unveiling marvelous vistas, the great majority of their colleagues are either blissfully unaware of this work or they take active opposition to it. For the parallel universe (or gap) maintained by the Blindspot exists within the scientific community just as stubbornly as it does within the general public. While those on the far end of the bell-curve distribution of explorers chip away at the Blindspot, those in the middle find it not just irrelevant, but downright threatening.

Because in a certain deep, existential sense, it is.

Not that I'm out to convert anyone to my way of thinking. Sure, this perspective may offer a particular view on the root causes of human suffering, but if that were held in a problematic context, it would be buying into the same structures of mind to which it stands in contrast. Rather, as long as I can help anyone gain some awareness of the option that exists in the heart of the Spot, and give it a fair inspection, that's good enough for me. The thing is then exposed, whether or not anybody follows where it points. Consider this a mere invitation to look for yourself, if you're so inclined. The concepts presented here are meant to be wrestled with in your own personal style, never swallowed whole as received gospel.

I'm also not out to convert anyone, because in any individual's case there may be some damn good reasons why they might be wise to stay put just where they are, wherever it may be along the religio-spiritual spectrum. The truth may be the same for everybody, yet strangely, its actual realization in any lifetime may not be. The consequences may be painful for both person and planet, but as for the truth itself...

Not only are the stakes not high, they do not even pertain.

Or not quite. Suppose, for example, that we invoke the image of Divine Mother, one common representation of Truth, the world over. From Her perspective, the stakes under consideration here are moot. Yet...and yet, they cannot be dismissed, either. For the tears She sheds for us come from eyes that do not water. The heartbreak She feels for us come from a heart that remains whole and radiant. The embrace She would gladly enfold us within come from arms that only await. And they can await for an eternity, for to Her there is no such thing as time, but only Now.

The stakes for you, me, and planet couldn't be higher. The stakes for the truth of who we really are, whatever its holy personifications, are nil. And the relationship between That and us—that is our concern in the pages to come. The tea-servers stand poised at the Tavern of Paradox we are about to enter. Careful now, don't trip; the threshold is invisible.

II

EXOTERICA/ESOTERICA

Here's the spoiler (so close your eyes): The Blindspot hides within the spiritual domain which can be labeled the "esoteric."* And the "gap" is that which yawns between this domain and the one which can be labeled "exoteric."

Among the folks involved with things exoteric—the vast majority of everybody everywhere—there is little knowledge of even the existence of the esoteric, let alone any understanding of it. This is the case even though adherents of various forms of esoteric spirituality probably number in the millions (or at least dozens). It's as if there were a one-way window nested in the gap between these two parallel universes. The adherents of things esoteric possess a good understanding of most things exoteric; they have the capacity to peer through the glass. Most of them, after all, have spent some earlier time on the exoteric side and have personal experience with it. While the reverse is not the case; those on the exoteric side cannot see through the glass and are mostly unaware of the other side.

Given the explosion of all manner of Web-based and video-based and book-based teachings out there today, the world of esoteric wisdom has never been more widely available to the general public than it is today. Yet it remains largely unknown to the vast majority, who still inhabit the exoteric side of the gap. Or who, when exposed to the esoteric, instantly interpret it in exoteric terms. It's as if the esoteric is like the "third rail" of religion, too threatening to touch. As it is said in the esoteric traditions: "The secret keeps itself."

---

* Also known as "contemplative."

Which ancient truism may persist even through the 21st century, despite my humble efforts here. Which are aimed at whom? Well...

- Anybody who may harbor creeping doubts about his own religion, or whatever belief system gets him up in the morning and goads him through the day;
- Anyone who may have already glimpsed through the Blindspot, but is confused by the territory, for the label esoteric can be a deceptive cover for a wide variety of offerings; and these range from the silliest to the most sublime;
- Anybody who may have heard the term "nonduality," but may not be sure about what it means;
- Anyone who has reached the pinnacle of success in whatever worldly endeavor she has undertaken in her life, but who might still harbor the suspicion that there's something more;
- Any thoughtful person who might still be pondering how to reconcile science with religion without resorting to the facile crutch of "non-overlapping magisteria"[*] ;
- Any inquisitive person (or physicist) who has ever stumbled over the "hard problem" of consciousness[†] ;
- Any philosopher who has ever wondered (heretically) whether the 18th century idealist Bishop Berkeley might have been right, after all;
- Any inquisitive person who has ever broken a tooth over that hoary old mind-body question;
- Any public ethicist or advice columnist who might harbor doubts about the validity of his own guidance;

---

[*] See Chapter 13.

[†] See Chapter 12.

- Any biologist who might harbor secret (heretical) doubts about whether only pure, random natural selection could ever produce anything like a eukaryotic cell (without resorting to the facile crutch of "intelligent design");
- Anyone at all who might find herself wondering if the whole human game might be futile....

Among others. Yes, if there's one goal I set for myself here, it's to keep my pretensions modest.

The word esoteric carries the connotation of something hidden, secret, accessible only to a select, initiated few. While in contrast, the less familiar exoteric, when used at all, refers to something obvious, accessible, understandable by anyone. That's why the label exoteric has often been applied to popular mainstream religions. You believe whatever holy scripture is prescribed, you follow the ordained leader's directions, you memorize a certain catechism, you observe the holidays and other assorted special days, you follow a certain list of moral rules and you do your best not to screw up. What's not obvious about that?

In contrast, the word esoteric is often yoked to "spirituality" in order to convey a distinction from the religious paradigm. For the teachings that might fall under this category can appear to be quite un-obvious, indeed, if not downright obscure. Esoteric spiritual paths often appear deviant to the accepted, outer forms of religion. So there is a certain accuracy to the exoteric religion vs. esoteric spirituality opposition, although it's a tricky one and can take us only so far in this examination.

With its giveaway prefix, something *exo*-teric must also connote any path that looks to the *outside*, to external references, for its bearings. These usually come in the form of holy books, passed-down rituals, various foundational stories, priestly authority, and the venerable certainty that can come from the mere fact of all those preceding generations who subscribed to the same beliefs, some who cleaved to them under great duress. It is also the exoteric thread that is most intimately woven into the particular cultural fabric of its respective time and place, such that it is often hard to tease out one thread (the religious) from the other one (the cultural).

In contrast, therefore, the word esoteric must connote the sense of something whose posture is *inward*. Applied to spirituality, it refers to a path whose primary bearings derive from some form of inward-looking. In its purest sense, an esoteric path is one in which those things that are discovered on the inward journey take precedence over anything that may come from the outside, whether it be from Pope or Quran.

To boil it down even further:

The hallmark of any exoteric posture toward existence (whether religious or not) is *belief*. Any belief, after all, must be in something-or-other that is external to the believer. Believers (who are subjective) hold a belief in something imagined to be outside of themselves—an object. The believer (subject) *believes in*...X,Y, or Z (object). And there is no external object more magnetic to belief than this thing called God.

Which makes sense, because this is the way the mind itself works; this describes its dualistic operating system: *"I"(the religious follower) am "in-here"(the subject) relative to that Divine Thing "out there" (the object), which I believe in*. Makes perfect sense. Moreover, recent research in the areas of developmental psychology and cognitive anthropology makes a convincing argument that evolution has made our cognitive wiring predisposed to find religious claims and explanations attractive and easily acquired, no matter what the specific details might be, right from childhood, onward. As research psychologist Justin Barrett puts it, "the way our minds solve problems generates a god-shaped conceptual space waiting to be filled by the details of the culture into which we are born."[2] As a result, he called us human beings "born believers."

By "dualistic operating system" I'm referring to the only way that the mind can form any concept at all—by the (usually unconscious) comparison of opposites. The mind cannot even conceive of any "up" without some notion of a "down," for example; or a "right" without an inferred "left," a "good" without a "bad"—and so on.

Yet this is not the only kind of operating system available to a person. If this other operating system remains hidden—i.e., esoteric—it's only because the mind, with its dualistic OS, happens to dominate the lives of almost everybody. And thus the Blindspot holds sway.

I find it revealing that one of the most popular nonsectarian spiritual websites today is called Beliefnet. The unspoken assumption here is that spirituality possesses some kind of equivalence to belief. And the assumption underlying *that* is that belief possesses some kind of equivalence, or at least approximation to, truth. It's one of those "goes without saying" premises that has become invisible to the degree that nothing is, in fact, said about it.

Which is what happens when exoteric context holds sway in the land. Beliefnet is what happens when exoteric context holds sway in the land. And therein does the Blindspot grow fat, happy...and unseen.

Although there are some important distinctions between the ways that religions have evolved in the East versus the West, both brands are most commonly practiced in their exoteric forms—i.e., based upon beliefs, in service to the mind's dualistic OS—and are dressed in their exoteric garbs, woven into the fabric of their respective local cultures. And it is why the vast majority of people follow one of these exoteric paths. Either that or (especially in the more developed countries) they become atheists or agnostics or secular humanists or whatever—which are themselves all exoteric in nature. Any nonbelief, after all, can only exist in reference to belief; it's trapped in the same dualistic ping-pong that is the essence of how the mind works, the bedrock of exotericism.

This is a fairly important point, as exoteric religion or non-religion can *never* lead to Truth. Whereas esoteric spirituality—

Well, actually, neither does esoteric spirituality. But at least with the esoteric you're sniffing at the right, er...Whole.

Now, I'm not asserting that there's anything wrong with beliefs. Like any other human experience on the evolutionary spiral, beliefs will inevitably arise. Their production is what minds do. I have them and you have them, as did Jesus Christ and the Buddha. It is only when we take our beliefs seriously that we start to get in trouble. When we actually *believe* our beliefs. Or, in other words, when we believe the *stories* that we habitually make up about ourselves, others, and the world. And all beliefs can be boiled down to the stories that either we've received from others and adopted as gospel, or stories that we've made up ourselves and clung to for the same purposes—i.e., consolation, security, reassurance.

It is the mind's job to pass judgment on the impressions it receives through the channels of sensing and perceiving, and it performs this dualistic operation well. "This is good and desirable, that is bad and undesirable;" "This is right, that is wrong;" "I am smart; she's an idiot" (or vice-versa); and so on. Some of this self-storytelling can be useful as long as it's held lightly, within its proper domain. It becomes troublesome, however, when we convert it into beliefs and insert it into domains where it has no business being. Such as: the pursuit of happiness; the relief of suffering; the discovery of love; the realization of truth, however it may be expressed.

Yet it is precisely in those domains that people will freight their believed stories with even more special significance and cling to them even more fiercely. Indeed, it seems that the most praiseworthy thing that can be said about someone's belief in common discourse today is that it be held "fervently." And the more fervent a belief is held by someone, the more deference it seems to inspire in others (at least if it does not contradict their own beliefs too badly, when it inspires the opposite: warfare). Nothing is regarded with more veneration in today's postmodern, multicultural society than the fervency with which beliefs are held, whether religious or not. Our most powerful political leaders are elected on the strength of their "convictions," and God forbid (literally, in their own minds) that they should ever be known to "waffle."

After all, much is gained by this unspoken agreement in society. People can support each other with all kinds of mutual benefits via their fervently held beliefs—respect, consolation, meaningfulness and purpose, to name a few. Entire lifeways have been constructed upon the meanings and purposes that people ascribe to their lives, all of which are shot through with the narratives they have told themselves about what they regard as their personal journeys. And there's nothing bad or wrong about any of these things. Such stories comprise the life-support system for billions, providing individuals with feelings of security and solidity in an otherwise vast, cold, incomprehensible universe.

Moreover, to show respect for somebody else's fervent beliefs is indeed a hallmark of the Western liberal/humanistic tradition—and thank God for that! I'd be the last to disparage such a relative uplevel in human behavior, as far as it goes.

It's just that the entire context of belief is completely exoteric in nature. Meaning: outward-directed, dependent upon received concepts from external sources, plus animated by a host of conditioning forces, from genetic to environmental. And also signifying: dualistically framed, assuming a subject-object separation between the believer and the believed-in. Exoteric. And therefore having very little to do with truth. That fact is embedded in the word, itself: beLIEf. As said Nietzsche, "Belief means not wanting to know what is true."

And if you're reading this, I assume you *do* want to know what's true. And if so, you might consider loosening your grip on the stories you tell yourself about yourself and others. And about God, mankind, womankind, past, future, meaning, love, truth, spirituality. And read on.

> Oh, God help me! What a difference there is between hearing and believing these words, and being led in this way to realize how true they are!
>
> —St. Teresa of Avila

I wouldn't bother writing this book if I didn't know that truth offers gifts far more precious than any of the consolations bequeathed by belief. That in fact, the emotional and cultural supports provided by belief are ultimately shoddy and, finally, illusory. Could such consolations still leave *you* a bit, well, dissatisfied?

They were certainly not enough to appease St. Teresa. Yes, she had heard the biblical descriptions and they had resonated with her, but she had needed "to be led" into a deeper, more authentic way of realizing the truth of those words than mere belief could ever provide her. Many are the ways of discovering that beliefs cannot possibly be true in that deeper sense. Yet I find that even the most superficially apparent arguments often go unexamined. For example: If any belief were truly true, then any opposing or contradictory belief could not, by definition, also be true, could it? And in the realm of belief an opposing position will inevitably, *always* arise; it's the law of the dualistic operating system.* And then, all we're left with is 1) belief systems at war with each other (see human history), or 2) belief systems in perpetual academic squabble with each other, which although often amusing, can never arrive at some finally objective place, or 3) some Kissingerian brand of "mutual allowance" or "balance of competing self-interests," which although perhaps a welcomed historical development, is a fragile one at best (see the nation formerly known as Yugoslavia, the nation currently known as the Democratic Republic of Congo, the U.S. Congress, etc.). None of those options feels particularly true to me. I don't know about you.

When truth becomes couched in the conception called "God," the behaviors of belief can express themselves in some rather bizarre psychic gyrations among the respective congregations. These have been

* Is this not self-evident? Not only can the mind not conceive in any way but via opposites, but any "right" will always eventually beget a "left," any "happy" will always beget a "sad," any "up" will always beget a "down," any "electron" will always beget its twin "positron," and so on and on. So it goes within the field of manifest expression in time and space.

amply catalogued by the recent wave of scathing critics who have been dubbed the "new atheists" (i.e., Richard Dawkins, Christopher Hitchens, Daniel Dennett, et al). They have already emptied their magazines quite wittily at these behaviors, so I won't belabor their points here. Except to echo their argument that it would be difficult to imagine a mindset that has deployed more bushels of suffering, violence, and just plain idiocy than the belief in a personified God from whose lips spilled words (once upon a time) that brook neither question, nor any perceived insult. And the fun, these days, is far from over.

Yet although the new atheists have done a marvelous job debunking religion, they don't seem to realize (Blindspot) that all they're sniping at are the *exoteric* forms of religion, not authentic esoteric (or contemplative) spirituality. Which is why they're beating a dead horse, even though it's a horse that, God knows, still needs to be beaten. The belief-based scenarios under criticism here boil down to the presumption of some kind of separate, supernatural, undoubtedly male being (in the sky, perhaps?) who must be either credited or blamed for whatever events happen to transpire in the human realm. He may be praised for assisting the winners of races who win gold medals ("*With His help...*"), or saving them from injury that killed everyone else in the same tornado ("*I owe it all to Him for...*"), or matching them with their soulmate ("*First of all, I want to thank the Lord for...*"). He is rarely given credit, however, when that same professing racer comes in last or the tornado survivor expires on the operating table, or the lady turns out to be a tramp.

Which inevitably leads to the one philosophical speedbump most responsible for the shadow of doubt creeping into the minds of believers. To wit: If the God I've heard about all my life is such a loving, just, and all-powerful being, then how could He or She ever allow all the terrible events that afflict humanity to occur? Say, the Holocaust or the Haitian earthquake, for example. Or Mao's famines or Stalin's purges or the Sandy Hook shootings or the Ukraine invasion... *How*?

This confounding matter has been dubbed the question of *theodicy*, and has been responsible for more than one crease in the brows of theologians down the ages. It sprouts such vexing correlates as "Why do bad things happen to good people [namely, *me*]," and "What did I/he/they ever do to deserve *this*?"

But all of these rational gyrations refer back to the inherent weakness of exotericism itself. For, no matter how relatively liberal or broadminded a religious belief may be, it must inevitably rest upon some sense of a subjective, separate *me* (in *here*) in relationship with some external, objectified, personlike being (out *there*)—a being who can presumably act one way or another upon oneself, or others, or the world at large. If anyone's definition of the divine fits into such a conception, then the only alternative to belief would seem to be nonbelief, or at least second thoughts. The option of an *esoteric* relationship to the divine may not become apparent, especially when that option is missing from the common cultural menu.

Perhaps nowhere else in the arena of belief-driven religion do its fundamental fault lines become more apparent. To explain human suffering, or evil itself, all manner of conceptual overlays and doublethinks must be brought into play. The list is long: that people were given free will by God, and then misuse it; that God's ways are inscrutable and incomprehensible, and it's sinful to question them; that the cancer-killed child was "called to be with Him in heaven"; that the mangled mother was relieved of her suffering because God needed another angel to keep Him company; that the world, by virtue of its contrast to heaven, must have its own inferior brand of order; that suffering is God's way of testing our virtue; that the redemptive power of our suffering will be proven if we but cleave to our faith, because all our questions will be answered in the afterlife; that our suffering is just a footnote in God's epic battle with evil, His winning of which will allow the final establishment of His Kingdom on Earth; that every tragic world event happens only so that the apocalyptic prophecy can be fulfilled and Jesus can return and the believers can be raptured away; that "Tribulation worketh patience, And patience, experience, and experience, hope." (Paul, *Romans* 5:3-4)

Not even to mention that handiest of all scapegoats—Satan—with all the superstructure of belief and exegesis that have accrued over the centuries in attempting to explain *that* force and its malevolent influence in the world.

Young children don't buy all this convoluted conceptual lamination that adults press upon them in their desperation to "make everything all right" when Grandma dies or Dad disappears. The kids might appear to go along with such stories, but they don't really swallow it. This marks the beginning of the way we lie to ourselves, pass it down the generations. And these falsehoods carry forward throughout our lives, festering in our hearts, even while truth awaits discovery in an entirely different direction.

Funny, how the exoteric, by definition, was *supposed* to be clear and accessible and obvious. Yet the more rigidly it's held onto, the more convoluted it actually becomes. The more a person tries to believe it, the more doublethink it requires. Read those annoying new atheists if you want evidence. Try reading the Bible, if you want even more evidence. But the point here is this: *The tighter you cling to exoteric religion, which was* supposed *to be simple, the more complicated and muddled it becomes. Whereas* [punchline], *the deeper you dive into esoteric spirituality (which, by definition, was* supposed *to be hidden and obscure), the simpler and more self-evident it becomes.*

Yes, this applies even to that thorny issue of theodicy. Seen from the perspective of truth, the resolution that has evaded our deepest thinkers for millennia couldn't be simpler. Granted, it may not be the kind of answer they might have wished for, but that's so much the unluckier for them. Poor Leibniz would roll over in his grave.

Ah, but the punchline grows even funnier. The closer you get to capital-T Truth, the more *everything* will look topsy-turvy to the way you had previously imagined. Everything will seem to be the opposite of what it was supposed to be. But by then, you will not believe it at all.

III

ADAPTIVE VS. TRANSFORMATIVE

So, what, already, *is* the esoteric response to the question of theodicy? Well, the answer is precisely why all things esoteric seem so, well... *esoteric* to most people. So, it's an answer that will need to wait a few more preparatory chapters. I wouldn't want to spoil your suspense, after all.

One of the first things to understand about esoteric spirituality is that it lies at the core of every exoteric religion. The esoteric germ of the religion is down there, if you scratch the surface hard enough. For certain historical reasons having to do with their respective evolutions, you may need to scratch a bit harder on the surface of Western religions to find it than you do on the surface of Eastern ones; but the esoteric kernel will still be there. Even in the most doctrinally suppressive of Western medieval times, the occasional Meister Eckhart, Jalal ad-Din Rumi or Baal Shem Tov has dared to testify to that fact.

As for the great spiritual realizers whose words and actions inspired the resulting major religions, well, they did their best to communicate their esoteric understandings within the constraints of their respective languages, customs and cultures, but this was bound to devolve into exoteric interpretation over the successive generations of followers. As we shall see, the raw, unmediated confrontation with Absolute Truth (by any name), although simple, does not lend itself well to translation into normal linguistic terms. An often-used analogy is to imagine how a person who has somehow popped from a two-dimensional world into a three-dimensional world could ever return and describe it to her former compatriots, people whose only experience has been two-dimensional. How could the person thus popped ever convey what it means to hug someone? To pitch a curveball? (the second-best thing).

The accretion of misunderstandings, partial-truths, and outright falsehoods that must follow the death of any religion's founder is inevitable and has been well documented by historians of all stripes. The institutionalization of the faith is always built within the confines of political expedience, cultural norms, and two-dimensional translations. And its eventual orthodoxy is hammered into form by a succession of canonical conferences, military conquests, mass migrations, and charismatic personalities. To assert this regressive process is no big news; it's a scenario well accepted by all but the most fundamentalist observer today.

Yet the original understanding of the founder remains where it always was—at the core. And that understanding, although it may be couched in cultural terms very different from one realizer to another, is exactly the same. This is one of the central principles of esotericism: that there is only one truth and it's the same truth, wherever it is found and whoever finds it. The realizers may have their own particular (even eccentric) personality quirks, and will therefore communicate their understandings with their unique spins on it, but the truth that is realized by all of them is identical. And the individual man or woman who takes on the role of great inspiring personage is the one and only "hero with a thousand faces" throughout the ages, just as Joseph Campbell said.*

So if a person wants to find a path that's esoteric, one place to look is deep within his own religion, if he has one. In the words of theologian John Haught, you may be "drawn toward a dimension of depth" and may thereby discover that rumored third (or maybe even fourth) dimension. If you're a Christian, for example, even such seemingly impermeable stories like the virgin birth, the trinity, and the resurrection can be penetrated for their deeper esoteric meanings. As the last-century Indian sage Nisargadatta Maharaj said, the most essential ingredient for any seeker on any path (or no path) is *earnestness*; and if

---

* Or, as the Beatles put it: "the One and Only Billy Shears."

you possess that quality and trust it deeply enough, you will find your way, even down through the most exoteric of surfaces. This refers to a kind of raw *curiosity* to find out what's really true about one's existence, a ruthless unwillingness to kid yourself with any handed-down narratives. And given such a temperament, you may find in the essential core of even your own religion something unexpected. Although that's not the only place available in which to look.

Adaptive vs. Transformative: perhaps this is an even better way of describing the essential difference between exoteric and esoteric paths. As such, the focus of exoteric religion is to help people *adapt* themselves to optimal, ethical human living within the prevailing society they find themselves. It's about fitting in and fulfilling a sanctioned role in the society.* Which is certainly no mean trick, especially in today's rapidly changing, fractured, crazymaking world.

So, the adaptive posture is all about helping people become happier, more satisfied with their lives. And it is these criteria that are accepted as the most revealing about any path's worthiness. "Well, if it works for *you...*" is the remark often made when someone is evaluating anyone else's spiritual choice. "*If it makes you a happier person.*"

The emotional power of the adaptive promise is incredibly strong, especially because it's also driven by its secret sister, fear—if not the overt fear of not measuring up, then the more covert fear (the fear underlying all fears) of nonexistence. Except that none of the above—neither the rewards of adaptiveness nor its flip-side punishments—has anything to do with the truth. Ultimately, even the adaptive posture

---

* Which, incidentally, also renders a population much easier to govern, and which is why the separation of church and state is such a rarity in history—such a radical proposition and so difficult to achieve and maintain.

is not so adaptive, after all. As said the noted psychiatrist R.D. Laing (sometime late in the last century):

> Society highly values its normal [adapted] man. It educates children to lose themselves and to become absurd, and thus to be normal. Normal men have killed perhaps 100,000,000 of their fellow men in the last fifty years.[3]

By contrast, the esoteric approach is utterly, annihilatingly... *transformative*, and has only an incidental, derivative relationship to adaptiveness—or even happiness, for that matter. Thus the distinction, again, between exo- and eso-teric. For although an esoteric path can indeed point toward the ultimate key to the relief of human suffering, that is merely a kind of byproduct of it. The path inward is a path leading toward the Unknown, and the result may or may not be adaptive, whatsoever. The price tag reads "Satisfaction Not Guaranteed." That's just not its concern, so the attached warning label should be noted.*

This caution points to a major reason why the not-necessarily-adaptive posture fails to attract much popular support, for the transformative aspirant needs to want truth more than he desires comfort; needs to yearn for beauty more than she wants consolation; needs to have his heart set on love more than he craves satisfaction. A double irony here: 1) That the so-called love and beauty usually sought do not hold a candle to the genuine articles going by the same name that are ignored; and 2) That these ultimate values are already resident in every single human being alive, already percolating deep down inside, and yet entire lifetimes can be spent in the (usually unconscious) overlooking of them.

---

* Sure, the awakened individuals with which I am acquainted have all been highly functional, joyful people. But their passion for truth was never predicated upon such an unguaranteed outcome, only for the thing itself, however it turned out.

If we start to look beyond strictly exoteric paths, we might encounter systems that can be categorized as New Age or New Thought paths. These represent the first stop that many seekers make when they dip their toes into nontraditional religions. Although these can represent a gesture towards the esoteric, they actually carry just more subtle forms of adaptive strategy in the end.

Broadly speaking, New Age paths can be recognized by their focus on the mind and its habits of thought (dangling participle notwithstanding). Insofar as this is the case, they do indeed represent a step inward—a recognition that the human "problem" is not answerable by external authority or handed-down doctrine. To one degree or another—and we are describing a spectrum of teachings here—such paths guide their adherents toward recognizing when they've fallen into negative thought patterns, so they can then consciously change them into positive ones. In such congregations you hear a constant drumbeat of reminders to keep your thoughts on the brighter side of life—indeed, "positive affirmations" are one of the hallmarks of this spiritual context.

This positivity is usually expressed and affirmed in the areas of self-esteem, self-image, good health and prosperity, often culminating in something dubbed...[*drumroll, please*]: the Law of Attraction. This recent repackaging of the perennial psychic flimflam, centuries old, preys on fairytale yearnings we never seem to entirely grow up out of (*May I be loved; may I prosper; may I live long*); and the emotional argument it makes is tremendously, um, *attractive.*

As the New Age argument goes: Since God Himself, if He is anything, must be loving and whole and creative and obeying of no limitations...and since you are an expression of That, a true child of God (or Higher Power or Source or Goddess)...then to align one's mind with that power must unleash that same energy in you. Change your thinking to the positive, align your mind with the higher good, visualize what you desire, affirm that you *deserve* this desire...and it shall become so. Is indeed *already* so.

There is a germ of truth in this belief posture. The adherents are on the right track, although the continuum of New Age expression runs from the easily-parodied (candles, incense, pyramids, priestly garments, pentagramatic altars) to the more sober. One critic has called such paths "religion purged of religion." And while this description might not fit all New Age paths, it definitely describes the far end of the range, such as the phenomenon known as Sunday Assemblies—"a church for people who don't believe in God"—where folks just gather together to belt out pop songs and feel all communal about it.

At the other end of the New Age continuum, however, where people do exercise some rigor about looking at their own minds and how they work, the fragrance of something else can be sensed, a bouquet from behind the Blindspot. Yet even here, the Spot itself remains quite unseen. As the troublemaking psychologist Brad Blanton has put it:

> The power of positive thinking is the biggest load of bullshit of our day. With positive thinking and affirmations, we start from an image of ourselves as flawed, and try to use thinking as a strategy to make ourselves whole. [But] thinking is not the source of power. *Being* is the source of power. And in being, we are already whole.[4]

Although this quote may include some notions we haven't yet defined, it's a kind of foretaste, a hint of the Blindspot; and maybe already you can sense something about where this rhetorical river is headed.

One more definitional refinement, before proceeding further down the esoteric rabbit hole: *An exoteric, adaptive path refers to any process of existential enquiry or ritual that yields answers, ultimately consoling ones; whereas esoteric, transformative paths refer to any process of existential enquiry or ritual that yields only more questions, ultimately frustrating ones.*

So it is that even New Age path followers, as nontraditional as they may imagine themselves to be, sit firmly in the consoling camp. To be affirmed (and re-affirmed) that your mind-mediated co-creativity with God entitles you to the fulfillment of your desires, represents a supremely consoling philosophy, does it not?

Moreover, as we shall see, New Age paths, despite how holy some of their language may be, are all about the fulfillment of a self that the esoteric paths do not even recognize as existing, as such. Even if their attracting programs *could* boost results within the domains of career, health, money, sex, and success (a dubious assertion, at best), such results would inevitably unfold into their opposites, given enough time, as every phenomenal event must, in conformance with the laws of duality. The esoteric search for truth has no quarrel with fulfillment, but demands first a clarification of just what *self* you're talking about. Whereas New Age paths are about mind-*training* (so you think the right thoughts), esoteric paths are about mind-*penetrating* (so you discover who the thinker actually *is*). In the end, the esoteric focus on truth and the pseudo-esoteric search for fulfillment are two entirely different animals, and ultimately the latter will fail to scratch the itch at the heart of the spiritual quest.

A word here about the wingnuts. There seems to be a certain psychological disposition, exemplified most floridly by the American brand of apocalyptical fundamentalist Christianity, in which vast, hostile conspiracies are seen everywhere. Folks subscribing to this worldview detect interlocking networks of enemies and events prophesied in their scriptures, often involving extra-terrestrial forces, to boot. It's a view that detects sinister connections between shadowy international banking cartels, the United Nations, 9/11, the revelations found in Qanon, the nefarious doings of Dr. Fauci, the breadcrumbs of *Left Behind*, the ascension of Barack Hussein Obama to the presidency, and Area 51 in Nevada. If you don't believe me, just tune in to the right [sic] radio stations, wherever you may live in the U.S. (although other countries have their own indigenous versions).

These folks are worth mentioning because even in the midst of their paranoid delusions there does exist a whiff of the truth we will be exploring later: Everything *is*, in fact, connected. Nothing is, in fact, separate. They've got that much right. Even in the murky midst of their confusion, a ray of true intuition shines through. But a person's psychological conditioning will always act as an obscuring filter to his personal understandings, and the fringe conspiracy theorist is just an extreme example of this fact. Psychology matters. Everybody carries around her own idiosyncratic filter. As current neuropsychological research confirms, we do indeed see the world "through a glass darkly," tinted specifically with our own personal brands of preconception, not to mention neurological hard wiring. Nobody sees anything quite the same way you do; indeed, it's even debatable whether anybody else's conception of the color red is the same as yours. And much to my chagrin, nobody reading these words will get what I'm saying in exactly the same way I'm meaning them.

This principle is no less true when we speak of truth. The paranoid will get his glimpse through the lens of paranoia. The garden-variety urban neurotic will get her glimpse through the lens of anxiety. To quote R.D. Laing: "Both the mystic and the madman swim in the same pool, but whereas the mystic swims in it, the madman drowns."* [5]

Psychology does matter.

---

* A similar quote has been attributed to Joseph Campbell, but maybe they just borrowed it from each other.

IV

WHO WANTS TO KNOW?

And what, finally, makes a spiritual path transformative/esoteric, rather than adaptive/exoteric? Answer: questions. Or more precisely: *the* question. An esoteric path is one in which the only question that really matters, is asked. To wit: *Who...(or What)...am...I?*

Somehow, the esoteric seeker has eventually come to realize that the truth game is ultimately a game of identity—finding out "who you really are." They have sniffed out the possibility that the entity called *me* may not be what most people assume it to be. It is not what our parents told us, not what our society convinces us, not what our mind seems to be telling us in every moment. It's the most unsettling of all suspicions, when you start to entertain the possibility that you've been *pretending* something all your life (well, since about 18 months). Putting on an act. That you may not actually be whoever it is that you've been selling to both yourself and others on, for decades. According to psychologist Blanton, the crack beneath you opens "when you admit your act [and] also admit your ignorance. [When] you confess that you developed your act...in hopes of finding your way by faking it."[6]

Ouch. So opens the existential crack: When the *me* we've assumed to exist in the center of our chests, or somewhere behind our eyes...that subjective sense of *me*-ness that appears to be defined by the boundaries of our bodies...that definition of selfness that appears to separate *you* from *me*, and *me* from *it*, and here from there, and inside from outside...when we let in the possibility that none of that may exist in the way we have always assumed it did.

So, the essential, esoteric question is: *Who (or What) am I?* And a more frustrating question has never been invented. For that which is being looked *for* is none other than that which is *looking*. A mindfuck if there ever was one. But here's a hint: The answer to the question, *Who am I?*, is not something you can ever believe in.

Indeed, some clever experiments by neurobiologists demonstrate that our usual sense of who we are is merely a running commentary by the left hemisphere in response to impressions received by the right. And that commentary is fully made-up, inaccurate, and imaginary more often than it has any relationship to the objective impressions it is interpreting. It will do anything to give "meaning" to what's happening, irrespective of its narrative being trustworthy or not. It takes its job of lying to us, about ourselves, seriously.

Yet sincere esoteric-path seekers persist in their enquiry, anyway, because they have understood that without an ultimate answer to this question, any other consideration of self-identity must be moot. What difference could it possibly make what theology or dogma or philosophy a person might believe, assert, cleave to, or practice, after all, if he or she doesn't even know, for starters, who they *are*? And if they can't be sure about who *they* are, then it also calls into question who all those apparent other people, out there, might be. And then ultimately: what is the actuality of *all* those apparent other things, out there, out and out, as far *out* as it's possible to go?

That the fundamental question of self-identity must take primacy in any spiritual path might seem too obvious to mention, were it not for the fact that 98.6 percent* of the available paths alleging to be spiritual, miss it entirely—which is nothing if not emblematic of the Blindspot. It could be said, in fact, that the foundational blind spot of humankind is the false assumption that who-you-are is exclusively defined by the limits of the bodymind, along with all its passing thoughts, feelings, sensations and perceptions. It is the mother of all blind spots, out of which every other possible error—every affliction—in humanity's long crawl from the primordial swamp, has arisen.

---

* By my careful calculations.

Firmly entrenched within exotericism, this mistaken conclusion about self-identity may be an unavoidable consequence of our cultural conditioning, a secondhand inference we make, reinforced by everyone, everywhere we look. But to be clear, the question "Who am I?" is not meant to refer to your *sense* of selfness—your thoughts, feelings, memories, talents, neuroses...nor your roles as parent, child, doctor or burger-flipper...nor your gender or sexual orientation...nor your political, ethnic or national affiliations...nor any of your particular eccentricities and idiosyncrasies. There's nothing amiss about possessing a sense of selfness with regard to any of these things. Yet if the *sense* of selfness is not eventually distinguished from an *actual* self, it will only serve to thicken the veil of illusion. And if that veil is not seen through as part of our maturing process into adulthood—both spiritual and otherwise—it renders all other considerations about life and the universe moot.

If you consider the horizontal line of a cross to represent lateral progression through life, this could be seen as the adaptive/exoteric movement—the domain of psychological healing, self-help techniques, normal developmental maturing, conventional success. Such is the domain where the "me," as defined by body and psyche, holds sway, and possesses its own reality and significance. It's the vertical line, however, that lends depth and profundity to the lateral movement. And it's on this axis where one's definition of that selfness undergoes a radical re-evaluation. But the transformative magic occurs only where the intersection of the two axes meet.* Where they meet does not come without a certain tension, however, as the following examples illustrate.

"I accept So-and-So as my personal Savior." The question, "personal to *whom*?" does not even arise along the lateral axis. The identity of the self goes unquestioned because it's just assumed as obvious: It's *me*: Tony or Antonia or Antonio or LaTonya.

---

* This is one way that the Christian cross has been interpreted through an esoteric lens, and is not original with me. Where the horizontal and vertical axes meet, the perceptions of duality are swallowed up by the recognition of nonduality—but also vice-versa, giving rise to the "enlightened duality" discussed in Chapter 17.

"I will be washed of my sins if I prostrate myself towards Patagonia five times a day." The question of who should take responsibility for the commitment of these so-called sins does not arise along the horizontal line. Not to mention: What manner of divinity could possibly exist in Patagonia—or even Temple Mount—that does not exist anywhere else?

"I believe in the law of attraction." Attraction to what/whom?—this is not examined. Not to mention: What is it about this *me* of yours that is incomplete just the way it is—that needs something else to be attracted to it in order to be fulfilled?

"I am the captain of my ship, in control of my life." A comforting illusion, perhaps, but: Who is this skipper kidding?

"This life of mine is merely preparation for the afterlife, where I can collect my reward (and rejoin all my loved ones)." Never wondered: Whose life are you living right *now*, as this body? And what was living you *before* you appeared as this body now? (Famous Zen riddle: *Who were you before your mother was born?*)

"I believe that the soul is immortal." Never asked: *Whose* soul? What is the nature of any such individualized, separate, self-existent entity that may or may not move on after this appearance?

"I must wage holy war, jihad, *against the infidel."* Never examined: Who is the actual opponent to anybody who really desires to serve God? Who is the real infidel in the room?

"But my identity as Black [or Gay or Serbian or Orthodox or Democrat...] is very important to me; and I want everybody else to accept me as I am." No argument here, as far as it goes. Yet where is the peace and contentment found in all these strident demands for recognition for an identity whose boundaries have not been explored beyond the horizon of skin? Whither whirled peas?

No small matters, all these. For any religion or spiritual path (or no path at all) that fails to bring the seeker to a confrontation with her self-identity cannot possibly lead her to the doorway of truth. And must instead therefore lead her straight (or crookedly) into the domain of what the Buddha called (in rough translation) *unsatisfactoriness*—a sense that may be felt anywhere on a continuum ranging from niggling anxiety to, well, you know: depression, despair, misery. Along with their tethered cousins: jealousy, hate, avarice, anger, fear, deceitfulness...self-distrust, self-dishonesty, self-sabotage...

Such is the inevitable consequence when you hew close to the horizontal axis alone and imagine yourself to be no more than what you look like to others—just one more object among eight billion similar objects, each one intrinsically existing as a separate self, and all of whom imagining themselves as tiny, helpless beings, arrayed against an incomprehensibly cold, vast universe, in which each entity must strive to snatch his own little piece of security in competition with all the others with similar aims—or die trying. Innocently buying into this majority view that we were conditioned into by our parents and society, we become mired in a body and possessed by a mind, alienated from a world we feel powerless to control, hopelessly insignificant in a cosmos too vast to conceive. Such is a recipe for suffering, both individual and collective.

The terms "enlightened" or "awake" or "realized" have often been used to describe individuals who have answered this identity question for themselves—who have realized their "true nature" and have *found* what all this seeking has been about. And a certain percentage of these individuals go on to assume the role of teacher or guru to those who are still seeking. And when that happens, spiritual schools or communities or s*anghas* (Sanskrit) often spring up around them.

Such teacher-figures are not to be confused with ordinary priests, rabbis, pastors or imams, as these folks are not generally regarded as enlightened, nor do they usually claim to be. The phenomenon of spiritual teachers, on the other hand, is well-known throughout the East, a part of everyday life for millennia.* Although even in the East the

---

* Referring to the Indian subcontinent, Tibet, Japan, Korea, pre-revolutionary China, and the pre-modern Arab/Persian/Ottoman world.

major religions are often practiced in their exoteric forms, still there remains plenty of room within the accepted structures for the recognition and embrace of "enlightened ones" and their respective sanghas. So, even though the majority of Hindus or Buddhists, say, may follow their religions in an exoteric, adaptive fashion, they might at any time feel drawn to a particular guru and then be initiated into the esoteric, transformational possibilities available therein.

Partly because the practice of meditation is inherently inward-looking, and comprises the primary practice of all major Eastern religions, this transition from exo- to eso- is relatively seamless in those traditions. No problem.

Such is not the case in the West. Although there exists a long line of Christian, Jewish and Sufi mystics who have left behind brilliant trails of esoteric sparklers, their actual lives were often spent in furtive cover from the respective religious authorities of the time. Many were those who failed to escape either execution (of the most exquisite medieval variety), excommunication, or exile. The template may have been set by Jesus himself: *Dare to utter the truth and see what that gets you.*

In any case, this has not stopped the steady growth of the teacher/sangha model for the transmission of esoteric wisdom in the West. And in the 20th century this phenomenon reached a kind of escape velocity with the progressive waves of Indian, Tibetan and Japanese teachers who established schools in the U.S. and Europe. This phenomenon has now blossomed into all manner of locally grown products of the same pattern: individual men and women who have reached a point in their journeys where they feel called to assume the role of teacher for others.

Since many of these individuals started out at the feet of one of the old Asian masters, some of the new schools have retained the customs and practices of their respective foreign lineages. While other teachers have gone their own ways, assembling eclectic combinations of practice forms from all over in the best American fashion, making them more relatable for their contemporary devotees. And in an even more recent development, a number of these new teachers have burst upon the scene with no formal apprenticeship with previous masters at all, but rather seem to have stumbled upon the true nature of their identities on their own, by way of their own idiosyncratic collisions with Grace.

While some of these new Western schools have been kept small and intimate, others have attracted large followings, with ashrams or centers dotted throughout the U.S. and Europe. As can happen with any endeavor attempted by human beings, a few of the schools that have formed around charismatic founding figures have devolved into cults, while others have degenerated into enclaves of political gameplaying. Yes, this does happen. Some of the news about "gurus behaving badly" that surfaces from time to time in the popular press has been earned.*

Yet the following statement still remains the case: The teacher/sangha model has become the primary vehicle for the transmission of esoteric spiritual wisdom in the West; and the best of these schools maintain a high degree of integrity. The participants in such schools must number in the hundreds of thousands by now. Some of these communities have been founded by men and women distinguished in their spiritual understanding and ability to communicate it to their audiences. By now there should be nothing new or strange or *woo-woo* about this phenomenon. And yet, the subcultural world it inhabits seems completely cut off from mainstream globalized society, where it remains invisible—except perhaps in certain unique cultural islands, such as Boulder, Marin, Amsterdam, Berlin, and certain crannies of London.

This wouldn't be worth writing home about, except for the fact that most of the quandaries that so perplex both individuals and entire societies today—that drive our debates, trouble our relationships, and keep us awake at night—have already been successfully addressed within that un-noticed psychosocial sphere of understanding. And have been addressed already for thousands of years. And if that doesn't constitute a Blindspot for us as a species, I don't know what would.

---

* The subject of what makes a "cult" a cult, and how it differs from a true spiritual school, is quite clearcut—but is beyond the focus of this book.

V.

THE TIGER'S JAWS

So to summarize: I have crankily divided the universe of spiritual seeking and practice into two broad postures: the exoteric vs. the esoteric. The former is characterized most fundamentally by *belief*, no matter whether pro- or con, and is aimed primarily towards adaptation to the prevailing culture. And the latter is characterized by an inward-directed process of enquiry, most potently by the question, *Who/What am I?*, the answer to which is aimed towards transformation.

Although one can find the esoteric germ in the core of all exoteric religions, the most widespread form of esoteric transmission, both East and now West, is the teacher/sangha model.

As previously stated, these spiritual schools, having been established by members of the human race, run the gamut of legitimacy and maturity with regard to making the goal available to aspirants—the awakening to truth. So, it can be a jungle out there for the seeker trying to choose among the available offerings; and by necessity I have oversimplified the categories. Yet it's also true that if the seeker has genuinely locked himself onto the beam of that awakening impulse, he will eventually find the teacher or teachings he requires, even if his trajectory may zig a little here and zag a little there.

For the purposes of my argument, however, my focus here will be narrowed to just the far end of the esoteric continuum—that place where the teacher is indeed an actual embodiment of the truth which has been realized. There is a name that has come into fashion (for better or worse) to describe that reality which an awakened being has come to understand, and that name is *nonduality*. So: At the core of every religion (if you scratch the surface hard enough), and at the core of every esoteric spiritual path (if you scratch the surface precisely enough), you will eventually come upon the same one understanding—nonduality.

We have arrived, finally, at my long-delayed punchline. *This* is where Blindspot hides out. This is where your true identity resides. And this is what the remainder of this book will be about.

"Nonduality" is a tricky term, however, and has been misused and misapplied so often in pop-philosophico-spiritual circles today, that some writers (the smart ones) avoid the word altogether. For the problem is that nonduality as a philosophy or a conceptual model possesses very little resemblance to nonduality as an actual knowingly lived condition of being.

Allow me to repeat that in other words: *Nonduality as a concept or philosophy can actually lead to more misdirection and delusion than any other model of spirituality, if it remains limited to merely the conceptual. It can only convey the vaguest hint about nonduality as an actual lived condition of awakened being.* This assertion cannot be overemphasized. But since we do need to talk about it somehow—and since it represents the focus of this opus—nonduality is the most accurate term I can think of,* so I will proceed to use it as carefully as I can.

For nonduality is really just another way of describing the ultimate nature of reality, the same reality that science, as we shall see, is currently tiptoeing around. And it is within the nondual perspective that the elusive answers I've been alluding to up till now, lie. And although not exactly common, nondual teachers and schools are not nearly as rare today as you might imagine. Nondual books proliferate on Amazon booklists, and videos of nondual teachers are deployed fruitfully on

---

* Owing its source to the Sanskrit term, *Advaita*, meaning "not two"—a designation certainly more to the point than such obscurations as "panpsychism" or "pantheism" or "panentheism."

YouTube. Where in centuries past the scrawny aspirants had to trek hundreds of miles and climb to mountaintop caves in order to find their teachers, today (for better or worse) the entire nondual chattersphere is available to the curious at the click of a mouse. The nondual truth is hidden in plain sight, right in the heart of the Blindspot.

Ah, so the time has come to reveal the great nondual secret. And I shudder to tell. When confronted with the same challenge, after all, all those major dudes of spiritual history had the same problem. As stated previously, the mind itself runs on a dualistic operating system, and its language (no matter whether called English or Tagalog) is dualistic in structure. So the masters usually went "meta" with their efforts to communicate. By the very nature of that which they realized, they were forced to merely make allusions to it, give hints about it, cock their heads and wink their eyes. They told parables, offered metaphors, made riddles. Got all cosmic and stony. Described what it was *not*, rather than what it *was* (in Christian theology, *Via Negativa*). Seemed to go around in circles, forever contradicting themselves.

All of which is quite understandable. For what do you get when you scratch deeply enough through all the layers of belief, doctrine, conceptual framework? What do you get when you explode the exoteric structure, then exhaust the esoteric search? In all places, at all times, by all realizers, here's what you get:

[*insert* Silence *here*]

Yet in their many endearing (compassionate) attempts to express it to their respective publics, and perforce put a name to it, they called this ultimate, nondual *blank*...Truth or Reality or The Absolute. Or God or Spirit or Source or True Nature or Understanding or Humor or Beauty or Love or Being or Awareness or Consciousness.

As St. Francis is alleged to have said, "Preach the Gospel always, and if necessary use words."

And as an anonymous Zen master said, "If I speak, I tell a lie; if I remain silent, I am a coward."

Whatever they called it, however, the realizers came into this knowing in a very particular way, *sui generis*, distinct from ordinary cognition. Like awakening from sleep—that's the analogy most often used. As if a person has snapped from a state of dreaming to a state of wakefulness. So, when a person came into this unique kind of knowing, he or she was said to have awakened to it.

To realize the truth is to awaken, and vice-versa; that's how it's often been put. It has also been called...

> to self-realize
>
> to be saved
>
> to achieve salvation
>
> to enter Nirvana
>
> to become enlightened

But all are referring to the same thing, the same quasi-culminating event toward the never-ending fulfillment of the human potential.

Those folks who have not yet awakened but aspire to, have often been known as seekers—a term often preceded by the adjective "miserable." With appropriate sympathy, the last-century Indian sage Ramana Maharshi remarked that such people were distinguished from ordinary folks by having their heads caught "in the tiger's jaws." What he meant was: This is a one-way street, and once you've turned 'round the corner, the reverse gear won't work anymore.

Whether we invoke tigers or the vampires that turns normal people into seekers, this might all sound quite ominous, and in a sense it should: the genuine esoteric path is not for sissies. It may be available to anyone at the click of the mouse, but that does not mean it's recognizable or even desirable. For if a person is really ready to discover his actual identity, her true nature, it will become necessary for them to let go of the identity they always assumed they were. In effect, they will need to "die" to themselves, psychologically and emotionally, and this is rarely an easy process. The transformational path is only for those who really *do* need to scratch that infernal itch, to finally yank that splinter from the mind.

Yet the actuality of realization is much simpler than any poor description of it could ever be. Indeed, it is simplicity itself. Remember: Truth is not a philosophy to believe; those are usually very complicated. Rather, it's a condition of being to be inhabited by you, yourself, firsthand. Which is why any beans I might spill here are the kind of bean whose spilling does not spoil the stew. The spiritual punchlines do not ruin the jokes. The discovery must be made afresh by every person alone, in a flash of nonconceptual insight, now and now and again now....until the "again" blows away like a puff of pollen.

Which is why they say "God bless you," when you sneeze.

So without further ado, here's a summary of a few nondual basics: The answer to that fundamental esoteric question, "Who or What am I?" is...*No Thing*. Having no self, no self-nature. That which had always been taken to be a separate *me* (as a psychological entity) turns out to be...*not*. Having no essential reality…well, perhaps in some sense real (as a contraction in consciousness), but not as a self-existent, separate entity. The self is like an onion: When you peel away the layers, layer by layer, you find...only more layers. No core. And yet you can't deny that you do exist. Who *is* that "you"?

This No-Thingy essence found at the coreless core of the imagined self is discovered to be the same in (and *as*) every apparent other, as well—every one and every thing. Thus, there really are no such things as every one and every thing. No *others*.

It is seen (by no one) that it's All One. There is Only That, Only This. Which is what you are, already, and always have been. "You are That, I am That, and all this is That," say the Upanishads. "All is the one, beyond name and form, and only God," said the Indian sage Yogi

Ramsuratkumar. Said and say all of them, all of those major (and minor) dudes.*

It is also seen that all manifest names and forms—all unique and different people and animals and plants and rocks—are also, simultaneously, not other than that same No-Thingy suchness. In all times, conditions, places, circumstances...there is Only One Happenstance ever going on, Only One Simplicity, whether active and manifest in creation (*Shakti, Prakriti, Spirit*) or unmanifest, as infinite potential (*Shiva, Purusha, Logos*).

Existence is therefore nondual—not two (*Advaita*). And nonduality is the existential, philosophical, spiritual, and scientific understanding of non-separation and fundamental oneness. "A physicist is just an atom's way of looking at itself," said quantum pioneer Niels Bohr.

Although a person may certainly retain a *sense* of selfhood, appropriate for maintaining the survival of the biological machine, this is entirely different from identifying with a psychological *me*-ness, which, when examined closely, turns out to be imaginary. Nonduality is the understanding that one's personal attachment to, and identification with, all the common dualisms imagined by mind, is the mechanism that maintains the Blindspot and avoids the void of reality.

The trickiest part of all this nondual blather is that this All One Whatever cannot be a "thing," not any kind of personage, not an "it." If it were an "it," after all, then there would have to be something else with which it could be defined by or contrasted to. But because our language is based upon the dualistic paradigm of subject/object, we can't really nail it with words. Indeed, we can't even *think* in any way other than dualistically. Just try it. Try to imagine an up without a down; a left without a right, etcetera.

This is why nondual teachers are forever cautioning the seeker against trying to reduce this All One (no)Thing to a concept. It's not

---

* Apologies to Steely Dan.

because the seeker isn't smart enough; it's because the mind is simply not the appropriate tool for this task. Even a statement such as "all things are one" creates an instant distinction between one and not-one (many). It's hardly any wonder that nonduality can be so easily misunderstood. It's simply not within the mind's domain to understand; and if it's not within the mind's domain, then it must also be something beyond belief.

It *is* beyond belief. Which is precisely what keeps it so neatly hidden in the Blindspot.

One conceptual gimmick that's often used by nondual teachers is to ask us to imagine that this One (no)Thing is That in which all apparent things arise—every thought, emotion, sensation and perception. Indeed, the same *me* we imagine ourselves to be is nothing other than the play of all those elements arising, abiding for a while, then passing away in That which you actually are—whatever that is. Even the most sublime mystical experiences only arise (and dissolve) in That—which is why no experience, no matter how expanded or mind-blowing it may be, is not considered as having any fundamental significance on the path.

Ultimately, not even those things—thoughts, sensations, perceptions—actually *arise* at all. All apparent things, however gross or subtle, are merely the temporary patternings that the One Happenstance takes, while itself remaining unpatterned, unperturbed, whole. Thoughts, sensations, perceptions, feelings, chairs, trees, birds, moons, stars, galaxies...are all modulations or vibrations of that same One (no)Thing, expressing Itself, to Itself, as apparent objects. While remaining the unperturbed Subject.

In Buddhist terms, this is known as the inseparability of name/form and emptiness. The infinite potential couched in the emptiness, appearing as "the ten-thousand things." If we call that empty One (no)Thing "consciousness," we could say that all that really exists is consciousness vibrating at the frequency of any particular object. We might call it an object, but in reality it's just that singular consciousness modulating itself so it looks like something other than itself. God in drag. You might begin to see here how difficult this situation might be to put into words, which by their very nature insist on dividing things up into distinct categories.

Here's a sampling of attempts at the impossible:

> It's all nothing
> Becoming something
> While remaining nothing.
> —Adyashanti, contemporary, American

> Things are not what they seem to be,
> Nor are they otherwise
> —Lankavatara Sutra, ~4th century, Tibet

> The world is illusion
> Only Spirit is real
> The world is Spirit.
> —Ramana Maharshi, Indian, 20th century

> [It] remains constantly full
> And constantly empty,
> Both and neither
> Vibrating in absolute simultaneity.
> —Rajanaka Ksemaraja, Kashmiri, 11th century

> It does not exist.
> It does not not exist.
> It does not both exist and not exist.
> Nor does it neither exist nor not exist.
> —Nagarjuna, Indian, 2nd century

Please insert the name you call yourself in place of "it." There, I'm glad that made things clearer.

Question: How many nondualists does it take to change a lightbulb? *Answer*: Three. One to change the bulb. One to not change the bulb. One to neither change nor not change the bulb.

Disclaimer/Parenthetical/Interjective: When I use the term nonduality, I do not mean to place the "dualistic" in some irrelevant or lower order of existence. Relative distinctions—lightbulbs and those who change them—have their proper places in the realm of the real. It's just that most human beings live out their entire lives in thrall to the relative, and function according to that operating system alone. All of us are already quite familiar with that aspect of reality, for that's the aspect in which we've become conditioned. So, we know how confining it is, not to mention painful, whether within individuals or communities. It's the nondual aspect which is the *liberating* aspect of the Totality, and is far less familiar to us. But both the dual and the nondual arise out of that unnameable, uncategorizable Ground and have no existence apart from it. And unless you awaken to the nondual part of that holy union, you will remain in the common realm of confusion, to one degree or another.

So it's the nondual perspective that hides in the Blindspot, especially as is relates to *you*. As snarky teacher Jed McKenna put it, "The process of enlightenment is not about becoming who you really are, but about unbecoming who you never were."[7]

Among other things, "who you never were" is a someone who is looking for something. In time. Hoping to find it "in the future." But... (here comes the fine print): In fulfilling Nagarjuna's conditions, time and space must also be dropped. For here's another basic nondual understanding—that time and space arise only when there's a *me* for them to constellate around; they arise together as a package deal. In the words of British teacher Rupert Spira, the belief by the me that it is a separate and limited entity, and the appearance of the world (along with time and space) that functions independently outside that entity "are co-created as a seamless, mutually validating whole. ...As Consciousness sees itself, so the world appears. It is an almost watertight conspiracy."[9]

Again, it's back to *belief.* It's the belief in the separate entity called *me* that makes it appear as if there's an actual objective world out there, along with its features of time and space. The belief makes the appearance *seem* real, even if it ain't necessarily so. What makes this mutual congruence between a subjective *me* and an objective world such a "watertight conspiracy" is that there is no way for any *me* to break out of this hall of subject/object mirrors and still survive as that *me.*

But what if there is no actual separate, subjective *me* to begin with? What if there really is no such animal, except as just another thought, arising in This? Then there can be no time, no space, either; only nontemporal *Now*; only a nonspatial *Here.*

That's what contemporary teachers like Eckhart Tolle mean by Now.* Not a measurable moment precisely positioned between the past and the future, but something utterly else. Something unimaginable—literally. Now = Eternity. Out of the stream of time, entirely. This consideration of Now will come up again and again in any discussion about nonduality, so it bears emphasis. As described by Rupert Spira:

> Now is not a moment in time, sandwiched between two vast spaces of the past and future. This present Now is the only Now there is –the eternal Now. It has not come from anywhere and is not going anywhere.[8]

Time and space are fleeting appearances within the unchanging substratum (and intra-stratum) of timeless, spaceless Now and Here.

---

* Referring to Tolle's popular 1999 book, *The Power of Now.*

And this Now/Here is the only way out of the tangled hierarchy of endlessly reflecting mirrors of in-here self and out-there world in which the unawakened dreamers seem to be caught. In other words, there is no way.

Perhaps it is becoming clearer why, although the truth of nondual reality is simple, it is not easy for people to get a conceptual handle on. Each and every nondual highlight could be expanded to fill many large tomes—and has been. But for the purposes of this particular rant, here are the punchlines I've been driving toward:

- The seeker is already that which they are seeking, and they always were. Although the seeker will never find the sought, they can certainly *be* it. In fact they have never *not* been it.
- If you play the esoteric game of hide-and-seek, you will always be *it*. So, in the search for truth it's the seeking itself that renders the goal unreachable. It is, in fact, the perfect way to avoid that goal. Says American teacher Scott Kiloby: "You cannot do anything in time to notice what you are in the timeless."[10]
- As soon as the seeker starts to imagine they need to find something else or be someone other, then time and space and all sorts of other conditions instantly pop into appearance, and they are tangled up again in the endless circularities of the search. Continued seeking on this ticklish esoteric path only lends more solidity to the imagined *me*, even if it becomes a more "spiritualized" one, as in "I'm a spiritual person" or "I'm a seeker of truth."
- And the harder a person seeks, the more she bears down, the more solid her sense of *me* becomes. The entire game becomes more and more futile: How can the eye see itself? How can the self attain what it always already *is*?

If the spiritual goal, so to speak, is to realize the empty, or insubstantial, nature of the personality-self—and ultimately, the no-selfness of the inexpressible—then this is something that that same self cannot do. For the self is capable only of reinforcing the idea of its own solid, separate existence—or recoiling from its dissolution.* Yet if we've got our head caught in the tiger's jaws, we've got to keep trying anyway; we're compelled by the wrench of our most primal yearning. What other choice do we have?

Can you see the special nature of esoteric spiritual seeking, as contrasted to every other kind of seeking? Predictably, the typical human seeker will approach this brand of seeking the same way as any other kind of seeking, with the same kit of psychological tools that she would apply to finding a job or buying a house or perfecting a skill. But it's a set-up. The entire spiritual game is a colossal set-up. For failure. The spiritual seeking game is the only game in town in which failure is guaranteed (if not wished for).

Who wants this? Is it any wonder that nondual spirituality is not supported by the common cultural consensus? Is it any wonder why it undermines the familiar sentimental context of exotericism? Is it any wonder why it remains hidden deep within the common cultural Blindspot?

Now we can see why so many spiritual masters have pitied the poor seeker and used such gory feline terms to describe his or her plight. And this is yet another distinction we can make between the exoteric follower and the esoteric seeker: While the former can actually achieve his goal, using the means he already knows or some marketing huckster can teach him, the latter, sooner or later, finds himself captured in

* In fact, this "self" is not actually a noun, anyway, but rather a verb—the very activity of attraction/avoidance or seeking/resisting—moving toward that which is desired and drawing back from that which is not. There is no substance to it other than this oscillating movement, to and from, back and forth. Hope-Fear-Hope-Fear-Hope-Fear-Hope....

the impossible binds of a tangled hierarchy, caught in an ever-reflexive Escher drawing, impaled by the tiger's sharp teeth.

If you're a seeker of truth, you know you're on the right track if going forward seems like a hopelessly futile endeavor, yet going back is out of the question. That's the sure sign of being on the right track: You're in deep dharmic doo-doo.* And you just can't see any way out. But then again, to paraphrase somebody who knew a thing or two about the subject: "He that is last shall now be first."

* Ancient spiritual expression (which I just made up), employing the Sanskrit word *Dharma* (adj. *dharmic*), which has been adopted in common discourse to mean, generically, any genuine esoteric teaching.

VI

THE T-WORD

But: Why do I insist on the annoying habit of calling *my* truth, *the* Truth? By doing that, aren't I falling into the oldest, most divisive (exoteric) trap in the world?

No. Allow me to explain (I can explain *everything*).

Nondual truth is not truth in the usual sense of that word. For starters, it does not refer to any particular position, or stand, and therefore has no argument with anything that *is* a position. While it may be so that, from their own, relative perspectives some propositions are undeniably true and others are untrue, from the prior perspective of Truth, both true propositions and untrue ones are both true and untrue at the same time.* In other words, nondual truth is playing on a field beyond mere relative truth or untruth—although, paradoxically, that makes it the truthiest of all.† Since its nature is non-conceptual, it is not capable of resisting anything that is conceptual. It could be said to be playing on a completely different ballfield of existence. Or on no ballfield at all. Or on all ballfields at the same time.

To compare the ordinary connotation of truth to nondual truth is like comparing apples to oranges. Or more precisely, like apples to apploranges. Or like orangapples to plorangaples. Or maybe—oh, nevermind.

---

* Subject to their respective perceptual positions, as discussed later.

† Which is not to say that there's no value to relative truth, which might come as news to the folks at Fox News. Relative truth and capitalized Truth are, well, close relatives.

There's nothing about nondual understanding that necessarily prevents anyone from calling a spade, a spade—or illusion, illusion. Yes, the essential substance—what in Zen they call "suchness"—of the most deluded fantasy may be no different from the substance of the most sublime insight. Yet the latter is far more *transparent* to truth than the former, and therefore much more useful to any aspiration toward love, peace, beauty, and the relief of suffering.

The goal of awakening to the nondual nature of reality is not the destruction or loss of any conventional concept or position, not even the concept of self or ego; it's only the capacity to *see through* them—to see their essential emptiness. To borrow from the late, influential American teacher Alan Watts, "We can use the idea of the equator without confusing it with a physical mark upon the surface of the earth."

Most theologies have their origins when somebody somewhere gets struck with an actual, experiential glimpse into some aspect of the nondual Whole—and then asks himself, "How the hell can I express this thing in words?" And then, if he's so inclined, he holds his nose and gives it a shot. Which then becomes a theological system, either with his own collusion or through the well-intentioned efforts of his followers. All of whom soon forget that it was only the first-hand, ineffable experience that ever meant anything, not the purported truths planted in the theology. One needs to believe a theology; one never needs to believe an experienced truth. After all, does it even make any sense for you to believe in the chair you're sitting on?

Another analogy often used (accurately or not) by contemporary spiritual teachers is that of Plato's Cave—that until we awaken we assume that the firelit shadows flickering on the cavern walls is the full extent of reality, not realizing that the sun is shining outside. So it is that in our sleep we see nothing but the polarities of opposites everywhere we look and assume that we must make a choice between them. Is it particles or waves (in physics)? Is it free will or determinism (in human affairs)? The process of awakening can be thought of as nothing more than the gradual (or sudden) realizing that every one of those apparent contradictory positions seems contradictory only with respect to their own partial views. And that all seeming paradoxes finally get resolved under the blazing sun of Wholeness, when we step outside. When we see that they were never contradictions to begin with, but only the result of fragmented perception. Firelit shadows on the cave wall.

The final result of any esoteric enquiry, when taken to its resolution, is as empirically proven—at least to that particular enquirer—as any conventional scientific result. Yes, this is a science of a different sort, one in which the seeker's laboratory is her own innermost sense of self; but her discoveries are blazingly self-authenticating, self-validating and self-evident. The term "self-luminous" is often used in the traditions to describe the nature of truth. Just as the sun both illumines whatever it shines upon and is itself luminous, so is your own true nature.

Which may sound like the most solipsistic of circular reasonings (as opposed to "objective"), save that every realizer in history, from wherever they may hail, has come up with the exact same empirical results (even if those results may be expressed in different culturally-biased languages).

And nothing prevents any realizer from announcing such results, if they're so moved. Although usually they're so moved only when encountering those who may be open to hearing about such things—folks such as you, dear reader, who has made it this far in such a strange tome. With others, the sages don't bother to waste their breath. It really doesn't matter to them, either way. Unlike the strenuous efforts of evangelical missionaries, nondual teachers couldn't care less whether you join them or not. Since they know that, in truth, everything is in perfect repose, why would they have any concern?*

* Indeed, from the nondual perspective all evangelical movements, whether Christian or Islamic, are nothing more than indications of deep sleep.

And if I haven't raised enough hackles already....

Since the Middle Ages (if not long before), people have recognized that human beings are simply not equal in their capacities to understand or metabolize more subtle spiritual contexts. This attitude may offend our Western egalitarian sensibilities, but it has found thoughtful advocates throughout history. As crude as the medieval concept of a ladderlike Great Chain of Being, all the way to today's sophisticated models of evolutionary spiritual development, it seems obvious that not everybody is on the same page when it comes to their psychological capacity (although *not* their innate human capacity) to grasp esoteric spirituality. Remember, the imaginary window between exoteric religion and esoteric spirituality is a one-way one, affording visibility only from the latter to the former and not the other way around. And it requires a certain measure of emotional maturity to move from one side to the other. Psychology does pertain.

And at the risk of sounding condescending . . . that's okay. From the nondual perspective, it really doesn't matter in the big picture. It might matter, however, to the individual person whose experience is one of suffering, and who may be seeking something he just can't quite put his finger on. It might matter to the person whose hunger for truth has just not been satisfied by the bromides of cultural consensus. And it might matter to the fate of this marvelous blue planet of surpassing beauty, called Earth. And that's why nondual teachers do risk wasting their breath. It's why some writers do bother to bloody their fingertips.

For, just on the fringes of both exoteric religion and atheistic rejectionism, there does await the esoteric, transformational possibility—abundantly accessible today from dozens of sources—even if it's usually hidden in the Blindspot. And who knows who may be ready to make the leap up the next slope of the evolutionary spiral?

VII

NONDUAL HOOEY

Just one more chapter of epigrammatic nondual blather, although this book is not meant to serve as a vehicle for specific instruction, per se. It's not a how-to book for waking up. For better or worse, we live in a time where nominally nondual guidance is exploding out there on Amazon booklists, through YouTube videos, via Zoom webcasts... You don't need another contender in that particular arena. Yet to understand the nature of the Blindspot, it helps to get a handle on the kind of beast we're dealing with here.

And so, the first nondual principle (once more, with feeling) is: TRUTH IS NOT A THING. The Thing Itself—i.e., the really real reality—is not a thing (or a Who) at all. If it *were* a thing, then sooner or later it would generate the arising of its counter-thing (per the laws of phenomenal duality), and then people would start arguing with each other over this thing versus that thing, and constructing great institutions around their respective things, and then maybe go to war over them or fly into tall buildings to serve them, and—

Hey, haven't we seen this somewhere before?

And because it's not a thing, the truth disqualifies itself as anything that can be known by the mind. The mind (which we can define as the medium through which cognitive knowing and emotional feeling occurs) can only conceive in terms of objects, and is therefore simply not capable of conceiving of anything that is not an object to it (the subject).

Thus, the truth cannot be figured out, not even a little.

Truth is the final, ultimate Subject, annihilating any and all presumptive objects. It is that within which—and really, *as* which—all apparent objects arise, stay a while, then fade away. This includes not only all the things "out there" in the so-called objective world, but all thoughts and feelings "in here," which, when inspected with earnest intention, turn out to be merely more objects, albeit subtler ones. For even thoughts and feelings arise and fall back into....

Who's asking? Who's looking? Who wants to know?

Truth is what you find when you penetrate the most stubborn, persuasive thought of all—the thought of *me*. It is what you remember when you step back through every presumptive thought-subject you can think of...back through the funhouse in which every subject-mirror flips into an object-mirror, which itself flips back into another subject-mirror, which flips back into yet another object-mirror....

....back and back through the tangled hierarchy of self-reflection, all the way back to the ultimate subject, the most intimate *you* of all *you*'s. Back to your true nature. Which was there all along. Here.

And which turns out to be empty of any thingness. Surprise, surprise!

Looking outside continues the dream. "Only looking within, relentlessly deep within, past and prior to the superfluous levels—intellect and reason and emotion and feeling and psyche and subconscious—to *What You Are*; only this can lead to awakening which itself has nothing to do with either without or within." (David Carse)[11]

The boy sits in the kindly barber's chair, looking at himself in the mirror on the wall, which faces the mirror on the opposite wall. Amazed, he stares into an infinitely regressing reflection of himself, with no end to it. Me-turtles all the way down.*

Peel away the layers of the personal onion, and what do you find? Only more layers. There is no tiny homunculus located somewhere

---

* Referring to the story in which the Western anthropologist asks the native shaman what he thinks holds up the universe, and the shaman answers, "a turtle." So the anthropologist asks, "But what holds up the turtle?" and the shaman answers, "Another turtle." So then the anthropologist, exasperated, asks, "But what holds up that turtle?" And the shaman answers (as if nothing could be more obvious): *"It's turtles all the way down!"*

deep behind your eyes or chest that is the seat of your secret identity. There is neither a "low self" nor a "high self." There is only no-self.

It is indeed "not this" and "not that" (as many traditions say)—but it is also *not* not this and *not* not that. The sense of self that's constructed by personal conditioning and cultural legacy cannot be simply dismissed as illusion, just put in its proper place.

It turns out that God or Consciousness cannot even be the subject to all objects, because any such über-subject must, itself, collapse, when it too is seen...*by what? Who? When?*

When even the subject to all objects collapses, the result must be absolutely singular. But whatever it is (which cannot be known), it's Only One (appearing as everything that *can* be perceived, felt, known).

It is the one "suchness" of all apparent things, including the thought of "me." And the thought of "others."

> From the point of view of a finite self, experience consists of a multiplicity and diversity of finite objects and selves, some of which are conceived as "me," others as "not me." From the point of view of experience itself, there is just the seamless intimacy of itself, one indivisible, unnameable whole, always changing in name and form but never changing in essence.
>
> —Rupert Spira[12]

It is what is left of experience and perception, when freed of all beliefs about them.

> He is the unseen Seer, the unheard Hearer,
> The unthought Thinker,
> The ununderstood Understander.
> Other than He there is no Seer, no Hearer, no Thinker,
> no Understander.
>
> Brihadaranyaka Upanishad, sometime before 1,000 BCE

Or, more contemporaneously:

> Thousand are Thine eyes and yet Thou hast no eyes,
> Thousand are Thy forms and yet Thou hast no form,
> Thousand are Thy lotus feet and yet Thou hast no feet,
> Thousand are Thy noses to smell and yet Thou hast no nose;
> I am enchanted by Thy play.
>
> —Snatam Kaur Khalsa chant lyrics, Sikh

> Whatever term we use to point to that "Thou" can depend upon what mood we happen to be in. We may call it God, if we seek to emphasize that it is worthy of veneration and appreciation, or Awareness, if we seek to emphasize its most universal quality, or the Light of Creation, if we seek to emphasize that it is a single dynamic field of energy.
>
> —Christopher Wallis, American teacher[13]

> Yet whatever we may call it, "It is the question to all life's answers."
>
> —Steven Harrison, American teacher

> It is what remains when you let everything that comes, come, and everything that goes, go.
>
> —Ramana Maharshi, Indian, 20th century

> It will therefore not die (going).
> Because it was never born (coming).
> It is that which is looking out of your eyes, right now.
> The simplicity of being...is the end of specialness. Except that there has never been any specialness. There is only this. There is nothing to compare it to. Even the comparisons are this.
>
> —Joey Lott, American teacher[14]

> It is what remains when you let everything you believe drop, and relax into everything you can't imagine. When the thoughts, feelings, perceptions, and memories with which we habitually identify have fallen away, then what remains is the essence of self, the pure subject without an object. What we then find is not a sense of "I am this" or "I am that," but just "I am."* ...You are not a being who is conscious. You are consciousness. Period.
>
> —Peter Russell, American teacher[15]

Imagine a bottle of champagne (thanks to teacher Francis Lucille and physicist Catherine Pépin, both French, of course). The casual observer might come to the conclusion that the bubbles are the significant thing, for it's the bubbles that attract the eye with all their motion and glint and sheer coverage. Yet the bubbles exist merely due to their contact surface with the fluid itself, which is the actual champagne wine:

> By analogy, our true nature, or Consciousness, is like the champagne fluid, while our forms—the body-minds—are like the bubbles, only existing fleetingly through their contact surface with Consciousness.[16]

This is just one of the many analogies employed by teachers of the nondual. There's the one about the characters that appear on the movie screen (the constantly changing appearances) vs. the screen itself (unchanging consciousness). Or the one about the film being run through the projector (the brain) vs. the light upon which the resulting images depend (awareness). Or the white light (pure consciousness) split up by a prism into an infinite variety of colors (the "ten thousand things").*

---

* Or as someone once told Moses, "I am that I am."

Or the many-colored threads (the multiplicity of forms) that are woven into the (one) sweater. Or the classic image of the seemingly separate waves on the surface of the ocean (the changing phenomena) vs. the ocean itself (that which the waves both appear *in* and are made *of*).

But all such analogies break down in two regards: The light of consciousness is not merely inert energy but is aware—in fact is awareness itself (which is aware *of* Itself); and . . .

All these manifest forms—characters, images, waves, colors, bubbles—are not only produced by the light of champagne—er, consciousness—but are *made* of it and have no existence apart from it.

Although experiences regarded as mystical may be cool, they are not what we're talking about here. Mystical experiences are like when the kaleidoscope of your reality has been turned part-way around (which is usually all to the good). But to awaken to nondual truth is like when the kaleidoscope of your reality has been turned not just part-way, but *all the way around*, back to where you started. Like those familiar lines from T.S. Eliot:

> We shall not cease from exploration
> And the end of all our exploring
> Will be to arrive where we started
> And know the place for the first time.[17]

Which makes all the difference. For at that point, you can engage with all phenomena, from the most mundane to the most sublime, but not be fooled by any of them. Take your pick of mytho-poetical references: The prodigal son has returned home (where he started), and is

---

* Buddhist expression meaning the vast array of distinct phenomenal expressions in the field of time and space.

welcomed by the father. You now see that the emperor has no clothes, even if everyone else pretends he's finely attired.

Just like before, you interact with people and things, but now you remain rooted in truth. You stay in relationship with people and things, but you *see through* the shadowplay it really is. You're the one in Plato's Cave not taken in by the flickering shadows on the wall—even if you choose to remain in the stupid cave.

Do I make myself obscure?

There is no agent or agency in charge of keeping us ignorant of our own nature. "There is no conspiracy to keep us in the dark." It is our belief in the reality of our realities that keeps us from noticing that it's a mirage. "We are emotional beings, and emotion supplies the power of belief." (Jed McKenna)[18]

The metaphors and expressions inherent to nondual badinage may not seem practical or relevant to everyday human struggles. And yes, they can seem a bit off-putting to casual inspection. Indeed, the dismissive designations "woo-woo" and "navel-gazing" are often used by folks with little personal engagement with esoteric paths, because they can't see the functional applications of such ideas to their own lives—or confuse them with gauzy New Age ideas. Even more commonly, however, this universe of understanding (this noosphere) remains completely outside the awareness of most people. This is so, despite the fact that, really, "there is no conspiracy to keep us in the dark"; and as I've said, proper guidance is abundantly available nowadays, if you know how and where to look.

Now, I am aware that all this nondual stuff sounds suspiciously like some extreme form of absurd solipsism. And yes, it does indeed share some similarities with that discredited philosophical position. We shall deal with that issue later. But please don't ask me if any of this stuff supports presocratic Ionianism or neoplatonism or positivism or relativism or monism or idealism or phenomenology or existentialism. This is not meant to be a book of philosophical dialectics. The nonduality of which I speak may or may not share much in common with Pythagoras or Aristotle or Spinoza or Descartes or Kant or Hegel or Heidegger or Wittgenstein. Don't know much about philosophy.*

Yes, I do possess a passing familiarity with some of the nondual flavors that have arisen in different philosophical schools over the centuries, and with how certain nondual notions seem to overlap with the ideas of the major dudes of Western thought. But although I may talk about the Blindspot in terms of ideas (and enjoy doing so), my primary interest in the subject is not in the conceptual realm. Again, nonduality is not a philosophy, even if it can be vaguely described in philosophical terms. And when the actual nondual condition of self-and-everything is realized for what it really is, then any ordinary decision or action that may arise from that condition turns out to be the most practically beneficial one for all concerned. And reveals the only one possible action that could ever have arisen in that moment. It reveals love (actually).

---

* Although I must confess a fondness for that ancient Greek philosopher Testicles, who knew a lot about the heavenly spheres.

VIII

WORLD OF WONDERS

There's a poignant scene in Vera Farmiga's 2011 movie, *Higher Ground*. The heroine (played by Farmiga herself) has been seeking her salvation on the path of Pentecostal Christianity. This is a path in which "speaking in tongues" is held in the highest regard, proof positive that Spirit has taken you over, that you have been saturated by the Divine Presence. And much to Vera's envy, many of her companions have already displayed that phenomenon, proof positive that they have reached the pinnacle of their faith.

So poor Vera locks herself in the bathroom and proceeds to try out speaking in tongues. She tries so hard to relax her own willfulness, yet still induce her mouth and tongue to somehow slip into that strange hinterland where they can be "taken over" by something higher, something greater and more powerful. Although reduced to frustrated tears, she does not succeed. Sure, she could fake it, but she has enough integrity not to; she knows that wouldn't be the real thing.

Aside from demonstrating a great piece of acting, this scene illustrates what I mean by the Blindspot in a particularly moving way. Not to pick on such an easy target as Pentecostalism, but the example is apt. For in the West especially, all manner of paranormal phenomena are treated with a mixture of fascination, attraction, revulsion and adulation. From visions of Mary to visions of Bigfoot, from likenesses of Jesus in tortillas to likenesses of plesiosaurs in Scottish lakes, from the appearance of personal psychic powers to the appearance of extraterrestrial UFOs...we just can't get enough of it.

Yet in the esoteric traditions, such phenomena are (once again) well known and catalogued, and have been for millennia. They even have names for the ones that appear as personal oddities for practitioners on the path. Whether they come in the form of involuntary tremors, shakings, posturings or vocalizations—*kriyas* or *shakti*—or in the form of psychic powers or superhuman displays—*siddhis*—such phenomena may certainly be noticed, sure, but they are generally regarded as distractions along with way. The teachings warn against getting swept up in fascination with them. *Keep going*, the teachings say, *don't get waylaid. That's not where the real treasure lies.*

I'm picking on the flashier psychic images as a way into a wider perspective on the Blindspot. They illustrate, first of all, how incredibly provincial we tend to be in the West about matters spiritual. Rendered flabbergasted over phenomena that, in the esoteric noosphere, have been known, classified, and expected for centuries. Worshipping appearances that, from the nondual perspective, are simply put in their proper places along the path, no more and no less.* "Provincial" may be too generous a term for us in our tickled fascination. "Immature" and "childish" might be more accurate.

We are paying a price for this immaturity.

Let's call that ultimate One (no)Thing, "consciousness"; many folks in the nondual world do. This is because one of the primary features of the One (no)Thing is that it is *aware*. Keeping in mind that the best language can do is offer weak metaphors, you might imagine that this aware consciousness discovers itself by way of its creations.

Then, suppose that…out of the field of infinite potential, a manifestation arises. Let's say it's a rock. Or a grain of sand. Or a guy named Harry. To carry the "discovering itself" metaphor further, let's say that the rock is the way consciousness "uses" to reflect upon itself

* It is said that when stigmata appeared on Padre Pio's hands (last century, Italian), he not only did not glorify or flaunt them, but actually felt *embarrassed* by them—the sign of a true sage.

the character of rockness, in the particular experience of that particular rock. Similarly, Harry is the way consciousness uses to discover and express itself through the particular experience of the person called Harry.

Harry is therefore also the way consciousness utilizes for Harry to become aware of himself— both as the rumored individual named "Harry," but most pleasingly (and completely) when Harry becomes aware of himself *as* consciousness. For at no time is Harry other than the very consciousness with which and through which it is making its discoveries. And vice-versa, whatever that means.

Closer to home, we can therefore say that the "arisings" of rocks and people are no different from the arisings of characters you experience in your own night-time dreams. Exactly the same. You consider yourself to be the dreamer of your night-time dreams. Who, then, is the one dreaming up *you*?

The nondual sage would suggest that consciousness is the dreamer of you. That you are an arising within the dreaming of consciousness, a manifestation arising out of the field of infinite potential so that consciousness may know itself better. And may appreciate itself uniquely, in the form of your own particular and never-repeatable expression of being.

This assertion by the sages may only be a story, but it's a pretty good one, as stories go. Ramana Maharshi employed the analogy that all such stories can be useful as "thorns" that are used to remove other thorns that you may have embedded in your skin. Nondual stories can be likened to the thorns that are used to dislodge the other, less useful, thorns that may be stuck in you. Even though in the end, once they've served their purposes, all thorns should be tossed away. Even the best of stories, after all, cannot encapsulate truth.

Since we all like stories, however—and some thorns can be useful—here's another version: Impelled by an inherent drive whose nature is utter mystery (although we can call it love), the Absolute (as infinite potential) bursts forth into manifest expression as the universe of forms—the "ten thousand things." And this bursting forth instantly creates the three-way split between the observer, that which is observed, and the process of observing. Which simultaneously conjures up what we call "mind," along with all its thoughts, sensations, will, memories, and emotions—everything that constitutes the dualistic veil behind which the Blindspot lives.

The point is this: If the nature of all such manifest arisings is dreamlike, then there are no limits or exceptions to what can be dreamt. Just as in your own often bizarre night-time dreaming. Visions of Mary or the prancing of unicorns or the howlings of Bigfoot? No problem! Walking on water or sleeping on nails or speaking in tongues or showing up in two places at once? No problem. I'm not claiming that any of these phenomena are real, only that there's nothing in principle to prevent them from occurring, since everything and everywhere is, ultimately, one and the same (no)Thing. And this event we call the "world" is far more multidimensional and wondrous than the average person might suspect.

> For me the world is weird because it is stupendous, awesome, mysterious, unfathomable; my interest has been to convince you that you must assume responsibility for being here, in this marvelous world, in this marvelous desert, in this marvelous time.[19]

So testified the Yaqui shaman don Juan, as famously recorded by his apprentice Carlos Castaneda. But he goes on to caution his student, as here paraphrased: *You don't want to get distracted by such marvelous apparitions. You want to get to the root of them*—a refined talent which don Juan called *seeing* (with full italicized emphasis). *And it is only then that you may truly appreciate this world of wonders for what it is, and even to dance with all its apparitions with impeccable wisdom and elegance. It's only from the vantage point of your true nature, however, that you can actually "assume responsibility" for this marvelous world, and not before.*

Of course, there's more to this world of wonders than unicorns and crop circles. There's also everything we call "bad" or "negative" or even "evil." As Castaneda soon learns, there might even *be* such things as demons and spirits with foul intent. Yet, since it's all the same One (no)Thing, no matter what its appearance, then these arisings too must come under the same divine umbrella. The same view must apply to every imaginable bad thing you can think of. The bad and the ugly cannot be left out. Cannot be cut off from the Whole, because the Whole is, well...*whole.*

Here we can get our first hint of the nondual response to the question of theodicy. For it is here that both exoteric religion and New Age systems fall short. By imagining that evil or negativity must be separated from the One Whole which is all-there-is, exotericism never gets to the root of the problem (which is not actually a problem). From the nondual perspective, the very fact that anything exists is all the evidence one needs that it *should* exist. "What is, *is*, as it is," say the sages.* And it is only the human, acculturated mind that ever tries to assign any rhyme, reason, praise or blame for that fact; only mind that would ever argue for or against the fact of anything being what it is. Which is why all human efforts to fix the "problem of evil," or to blame it on some other responsible party (i.e, God), have always failed to produce the desired results. And always will.

But watch out! For it's precisely here where the difference between nonduality as a philosophy and nonduality as an embodied, lived condition becomes most stark. As a philosophy, it can easily be misinterpreted to mean something like, "*Hey, Nazi concentration camps? No*

---

* Which bears no relation to fatalism, but merely the assertion that once anything happens, it *did* happen, and could not have been otherwise...but only once it *has* happened (see Chapter XI).

problem!" Or, "*Child soldiers and mass rapings? Oh, it's all part of the One Whole, isn't it? It's all the Same, is it not?*" "*What is, you know,* <u>is</u>."

Yes, it is. But even the most enlightened person in the world will probably display a different response to murder and mayhem than she will to rainbows and teddy bears. She will also display a different response to her own life difficulties than to her own life boons. The difference will lie in where she is coming from. As we shall see, sometimes the most appropriate (and holy) response to any given situation might be...who knows?—screaming at someone, tricking someone, telling a lie, abandoning a relationship, moving away, staying put...defending yourself and your loved ones in any way possible...even killing someone. Or many someones.* You can't tell an "enlightened person" by her actions, but only by what is directing or motivating those actions. What is her "coming from" place?

And to describe that coming-from place as compassion does not even start to do it justice. If peace is where you're coming from, peace is what you'll offer the world, irrespective of how it may appear. No need for commandments, idealized aspirations, or morality police. No muss, no fuss. Which may sound simplistic to the contemporary ear, but that does not make it any less true.

The nondual response to what we might call evil—the question of theodicy—is awash with paradox, at least from the viewpoint of mind. Yes, child abuse *is*, and is therefore not other than the One. Yet the most compassionate response to child abuse may not come from seeing it as a problem to be solved. Difficult as it might be for the mind to accept, the most compassionate (and practically effective) response may come from seeing it in an entirely new light.

---

* Even if they are your own kinfolk. See the *Bhagavad Gita*.

IX

DOING GOOD

In the song "Gotta Serve Somebody," Bob Dylan asserts that you're always serving somebody, whether you're aware of it or not. And that somebody is either "the devil" or "the Lord." And he then goes on to list all imaginable stations that a person might occupy in this world, all possible functions they might animate—but it don't matter in the least. No matter what your role in life happens to be, you're serving *something*—and it's got to be either one thing (the devil) or the other (the Lord).

Despite the exoteric language, that's not too far off from how it looks from the nondual perspective, although from there (or *here*), the view is a bit more nuanced. The thing that most of us are serving is our conditioned personality, often called the ego in the traditions.* Although it is unconscious, such service is not demonic, sinful or evil in any way. It's simply automatic, mechanical, asleep, that's all, so let's leave Mister Satan out of it, please. Dylan is a hyperbolic poet, not a sage. The actions we perform in this way are simply the combined effects of all the cumulative conditioning factors that make us who we take ourselves to be, the *me* we usually refer to when talking or thinking about ourselves. Our self-performance, our "act." When we take action, we are motivated by conditioning agents that are genetic, neurochemical, neural-algorithmic, environmental, educational, familial, genealogical (and karmic too, if that formulation makes you happy, though it's not necessary).

* In contrast to "ego" in the Freudian sense. The distinctions he made between ego, superego, and id do not apply in spiritualspeak. In that world, ego is ego, period—although the term can refer to a scolding aspect (analogous to superego) or a shadow aspect (analogous to id).

Again, this is not bad, plus these conditioning agents can also do wonders for your hair. We are conditioned from the word go by our parents, teachers, media, the overbearing pressures of society to conform...and there was nothing we could do about it. Nor would we have wanted to, in the normal process of developmental maturing. Yet as a rule we remain stuck in adolescence, never recognizing our robotic responses for what they are. And never honoring our potential for serving something else.

When on the other hand a person awakens to his true nature and takes action from *that* place, he has relinquished what teacher Wayne Liquorman calls the False Sense of Authorship (FSA). Realizing that his conditioned, named self is not the source of the choices he seems to make, he has become open to where his true agency is coming from. He then serves the Lord, however you may call it.* Such action is characterized by several giveaway markers:

- It is a spontaneous response to whatever is wanted and needed by any given circumstance in the moment. But the response does not come from any sense that there's a problem out there that needs to be solved.
- The action is not predetermined. It is not known ahead of time what action, among the many possible alternatives, will be the one action that is performed in that particular instant.
- It is action that comes from a place of no argument with what is, whatever that may be—even though any manner of passionate emotion may arise and show its face, even anger or fear.
- So-called negative emotions like anger or fear may provide energy for the action, because the One Whole can appear as anything whatsoever; however, such emotions do not determine what action is taken.

---

* Such a person doesn't necessarily know what he serves. He just knows that he is not steering the boat anymore; he has released the tiller and has left the steering to That which was always really steering anyway.

- Yet whatever emotion provides energy for the action, it comes and goes instantly, like the moods of a young child, leaving no trace on the bodymind. The emotion carries no personal investment, no Velcrolike stickiness to it.
- It is the one action that is in harmony with the way things actually *are*, as opposed to how things could or should be. It is in synch with the flow of life, sometimes called the *Tao*.
- Let's call it "enlightened action," for convenience. Such action will generally (though not always) look like something most people would call good. It will fit into most peoples' conception of what good means. But it will actually be performed with no regard for "good" or "bad," no regard for any external standard of ethics or morality, no reference to any scriptural commandments. And despite the rather dry descriptions bulleted here, this is how real compassion shows up.

When any action arises from a rootedness in truth, it will carry the flavor of reality itself. And it will therefore be the most appropriate action possible in the moment, regardless of what it may look like. If it happens to match any external standards or references of "goodness," it will be purely accidental. *This* is what true morality is. Not to be found within some specialized province of academic study. Not a prescription of rules, not a list of commandments, not the verdict from a debate among comparative pros and cons. Nor does it derive from some supernaturally God-given Moral Law. Yet any action that arises from it will be merely and precisely what is wanted and needed in any given moment. Pardon the spiritual clichés, but it will be the "right action" that arises "in the flow" or "with the Tao." Yet because it is completely resonant with Now, it cannot be known ahead of time.*

---

* Indeed, it is often said in the traditions that anything whatsoever that you need to know (if you're enlightened) only comes to be known in the very moment it *does* need to be known, and not until that moment.

So we hardly need to look to any one particular specialty for our moral guidelines, least of all theology or religion. And we don't need to look to science, either, as the new atheists recommend. Yet this naked morality is not relative, either. It is precise and absolute; it's just not knowable until the very moment of its application to the given circumstance. From the nondual perspective, then, all scriptural commandments, ethical guidelines, and moral ideologies are merely *descriptive*, not *prescriptive*; they are totally irrelevant to the performance of enlightened action. Even if they were meant to be prescriptive when they were introduced, all such behavioral instructions are now revealed to be descriptive. They appear to be more like "best practices" than absolute rules.*

The prescriptive posture is only needed if folks are serving their conditioning—i.e., their egos. When religious defenders argue with atheists, they always worry about how people would know how to behave properly if they lost their religion, with all its precepts and principles. If they lost the supernatural surveillance over their behavior that religion relies upon. But here's another example of the Blindspot: Such a concern fails to notice that any behavior that comes from the place of prescription is itself a kind of fallacy—the view that a person is nothing *but* his conditioning, which is not the case. And history abundantly shows that the prescriptive context has never been all that effective at guiding human behavior toward the good, anyway. I would pronounce it a miserable failure, in fact.

Another lesson shown by history is that when action comes from service to ego, within the context of solving a problem, it eventually produces the polar opposite reaction in the circumstance—if not soon then eventually, given enough time, per the laws of duality (again). Is this not self-evident? Any political "right" will always beget a corresponding political "left"; any Obama will always beget a Tea Party;

---

* Did Moses really mean "The Ten Descriptions"?

any military "hawk" will always beget a "dove"; any restaurant banning open pistols will always trigger ten others whose waitresses pack heat on their hips; and so on and on.

If a person's actions come from a place of argument with "what is," that polar energy will eventually trigger some manifestation of opposition to occur; you can count on it. Which is why no problem that we humans attack ever seems to be solved for good, no matter how noble our intentions. We hammer the bleb on the inflated ball, and a boil pops up on the other side. We win the Great War ("the war to end all wars"), but it only plants the seeds for the even greater war. We think we've finally put an end to infectious disease with our wonder-drug antibiotics, but this only gives rise to bulletproof superbugs. We put the brakes on infant mortality in country X, only to witness the desperate flood of starving youths drowning on the way to Lampedusa. Ingeniously, we find a way to power our entire industrial society, our affluent way of life...only to see the earth's climate come unglued, the oceans acidify, the seacoasts flooded. In the smoke of every righteous revolution float the particulates of the next counter-revolution.

This is what is meant in the traditions by "the wheel of *samsara*"; and we keep getting caught up in it, over and over. The hypnotic seduction of victory (the Final Solution) keeps luring us to action again and again, both as individuals and societies. And then we seem surprised when we notice (if we do) that all we've really done is give ourselves another turn on the *samsaric* merry-go-round. All of which epitomizes what I mean by the Blindspot.

All of this is fiercely summed up by the American teacher Lee Lozowick:

> You know the saying: "If it ain't broke, don't fix it." Well the Universe ain't broke. Every form of denying the Universe its need, or its urge, to manifest *as it is...* is an attempt to fix the Universe. Every gesture, when motivated by self-reference [egoic] over and against

> Universe-reference, is our attempt to fix what ain't broke. That includes service to those less fortunate than us, the healing of others, acts of generosity and social justice. All the "good" things we can do with our lives, when those things are defined by our illusions of separation and fantasy, are attempts to fix what doesn't need fixing.[20]

Which is not to say that if humankind suddenly switched gears and performed enlightened action *en masse*, this would necessarily solve all our global (and personal) challenges and create an instant (or eventual) paradise on Earth. No. We can't know *what* any enlightened action will produce. It can't be known until it happens. The planet could or could not be saved. Billions of people may or may not need to perish. To be awake is only to know that the results of any action are not your concern. You have released the tiller of your boat and have left the steering to the Whole.*

You've heard all this before. It's merely another way of saying *surrender*. Or, "Your Will be done, not mine."

Still, this may sound like a lot to swallow for all you planet-savers out there, until you ask yourself honestly about the way we seem to be headed now, the way we're going about it now. As long as we regard ourselves as individual entities, biographically-defined egos, separate from the Whole, cleaving to our "false sense of authorship," we feel ourselves always at odds with the world, in oppositional struggle against a seemingly vast, cold and arbitrary universe, out there. From that place, our social actions must be motivated by fear, no matter how subtle its influence or how selfless its appearance may be. So ask yourself: If these actions were instead sourced from a vision of reality that's

---

* Which was always doing the steering anyway, even when you were ostensibly "serving the devil."

closer to actuality than our imaginary concepts, might the results be any better? And if these actions were instead sourced from the kind of letting-go that I'm describing here (which is actually love in disguise)...would the results be any worse?

Here's the way Teilhard de Chardin (early 20th century Jesuit and paleontologist) put it:

> The day will come when, after harnessing the winds, the tides and gravitation, we shall harness for God the energies of Love. And on that day, for the second time in the history of the world, man will have discovered fire.[21]

Although it sounds promising, he doesn't say how such a dicey discovery will work out.

None of the above is meant to imply any recommendation for people to stop doing whatever they're doing, just because they may not be enlightened. Even if someone's actions may not come from motivations that are "pure" (free from conditioned mind), it would be silly for her to just sit around binging on the latest Netflix series until awakening struck her on the noggin. No, there is nothing in the nondual perspective that argues for people to cease doing the best they know how, solving problems and all. As Stevie Wonder sang, everybody should just keep on doing whatever they're doing, whether they be teachers or soldiers or preachers... "Till we reach the higher ground."

But in the meantime, here's how peeking at the Blindspot may help us: To not be fooled by the dripping sentimentality that the prevailing culture usually drapes around the doing of good works and the people who do it. Unless they are awake, people do whatever they do, whether so-called good or bad, as mechanical responses to their conditioning.

They may not be serving the devil, but they are serving ego. Which isn't wrong or sinful, but simply deserving of our honest looking, if we really care about what we say we care about.

"Thank you for your service"? Not necessarily. The motivations for any young person to join the military are legion (pun intended): It may be a tradition in his family; he may need the employment; he may want to fulfill some image he harbors about real manhood; he may hunger for adrenalin rushes; he may have bought into some story about patriotism; and so on and on. All merely conditioned responses to an imagined separative existence. Why should they merit such a maudlin pouring of faux-gratitude from the media, such shameless kowtowing of the politicians?

Nobel Prize winners are no different. And neither are the discoverers of cancer cures; the volunteer workers of NGOs in places like Haiti, Sudan, Somalia; foster parents; burn-unit nurses; Boy Scout leaders; charitable foundation workers, etcetera. Do they deserve our thanks? Sure, although with some clarity. To open a crack in the Blindspot means to shed a little more light on what's really going on—the conditioned actions of ordinary human beings, no more liberated than those of the homeless panhandler you pass on the street. To dissolve the Blindspot requires us to look with ruthless honesty, shorn of our usual culturally reinforced sentimentality. And when we do this about others, it becomes much easier for us to turn the spotlight around and look at ourselves. And to stop fooling ourselves about our *own* motivations and drivers. For to awaken to our true nature, we must also get ruthlessly honest with ourselves. And ask ourselves: Whom or What do *we* serve?

Okay, okay, so I told a fib. The unawakened person does indeed do what he does from the ground of mechanically conditioned motivation, yes, that may be so. But, that constructed personality, that identified *me*, is not *all* that he is. In fact, it's just a tiny aspect of who he is (actually even less), masquerading as the whole. It's an imposter, a usurper, a phony. And its veneer is therefore exceedingly thin, indeed.

So doth true nature erupt to the surface every now and then. You never know when. Maybe when the soldier puts his own life in jeopardy to save his buddy in the trenches. Maybe when Daddy holds his newborn daughter for the first time. Maybe when the woman makes love to her beloved. Maybe when Joe-the-plumber's son plays Bach at his cello recital. Maybe when the doctor-without-borders places an IV in the dehydrated infant. Maybe when the NGO-volunteer places the last brick on the new girls' school in Kabul. Maybe when an American president speaks at the site of a fresh Civil War battleground, where the stench of rotting flesh still stains the air, and says everything that needs saying in five minutes. Maybe when another American personage is called upon to speak at a massive civil rights rally at Washington's National Mall and tosses aside his script.

So, it's not so cut-and-dried. Yes, it's true that "you're gonna have to serve somebody." But the situation is not always all or nothing. Even the most "unawakened" person can perform action in service to that Whole Whatever. Although to do that, something must thrust him out of his own way. The *me* he always assumed was the agent of his actions (his false sense of authorship) cannot maintain its usurpation; it cannot pretend its doership anymore, at least temporarily, at least in this one aspect of his life. For true nature is always there, it's never not there, and it's just waiting for the chance to serve (and be served). And when I talk about awakening or true nature, I'm not referring to anything mystical or occult. After all, I'm only talking about reality. And deep down (despite its suppression in the Blindspot), everybody knows this.

In fact, blurry lines abound with this subject, and it's impossible *not* to tell fibs when trying to cram the truth into words. To relinquish one's false sense of authorship does not mean to take any kind of victim position in relationship to life, nor does it absolve one of any sense of responsibility for one's actions. Choices must be made (at least apparently), and those choices can be more or less aligned with some vision of kindness, generosity and compassion.

So, yes, you do whatever the situation seems to require of you, but—and here is the "higher ground"—you do it with the certitude that whatever you cannot do, for whatever reason, need not be done, at least not by you. And whether or not this means we actually possess what we think of as free will is another matter, which we'll tackle later.

Speaking of tackling, however: the Zone that's so often noted among athletes, musicians and actors is another way of referring to the "getting out of one's own way" that occurs when the FSA is dropped. There's just no room for discursive thought when you have to throw the ball downfield with four 300-pound guys rushing at you and only seconds remaining till they strike.

Suddenly, time slows down and the goalpost seems nigh; there's no problem, just the happy heave of muscle. There's just the shortstop's instant knowing of who is running to what base and how fast, just the skier's quick *gelandesprung* through the moguls, just the drummer's sweet surrender to the pocket, just the lovers' self-forgetful melting one into the other—you get the picture. It's a precious commodity, this Zone, and to slip through its gates is sought by all lovers, all artists, all athletes. Even though the seeking of it must be dropped as the price of admission.

These quarterbacks and presidents are not usually enlightened, of course. But true nature can and does shine through every now and then, usually in certain, limited sectors of a person's life, those areas that are freer of the person's conditioning than others. And that's the secret, for the conditioned self is much too sluggish to ever duplicate the split-second marvels performed by true nature. To get out of your own way means, literally, to allow the *me* to be dropped from your center of identity, so that Something Else can shine through.

Contrary to what might be imagined, such a *me*-dropping does not necessarily launch a person into some drooling, dysfunctional, transcendental realm,* but rather only renders her everyday human pursuits that much more effective and efficient. As stated by Lee Lozowick:

> At the core of real spiritual work is the possibility to lose self-reference. You can continue to do what you are doing (be a teacher or a nurse, for example), but let God work through you without any self-reference. Yet that's exactly what people are terribly afraid of. They believe that they will cease to exist if they give up self-reference. But exactly the opposite is true.[22]

So, as the Spot that used to be Blind comes into fuller view, perhaps we can better discern what's really going on—whom or what is actually being served—whenever anyone performs some act of social goodness, athletic prowess, or really, *any* act. We can see it clear-eyed, shorn of the usual blinders of socially-hyped emotionality. And then, if we sincerely yearn to realize truth, we can turn our attention around and look at ourselves.

Yet another common hook for our tendency towards sentimentality: pre-industrial, tribal cultures. Although it may be true that members of such cultures (generally) did possess a more developed sense of unity with nature and community than we do, these qualities did not necessarily produce kinder, gentler societies, and do not warrant the rampant idealization of them found in some "progressive" quarters today. For all the value that we postmodern folk may find in an appreciation

---

* Although admittedly, that can happen sometimes to some seekers along the way.

of these cultures, this brand of naïve romanticizing overlooks the many egoic drivers that actually ran these cultures, no more or less than they do in any culture. Once again, it's easy to fall into the trap of sentimentalizing here, and such nostalgia does not serve our own awakening to truth. Just as the sentimentalization of *anything* never does.*

Perhaps nowhere is this kind of discernment more to the point than in the perennial debate among philosopher-types about the existence and origin of human altruism. It's difficult to make the case that altruism holds any evolutionary advantage, even though Darwinian hard-liners strain to do just that. But how else can a good rationalist explain its persistence in all cultures? Could it have an originating locus somewhere in the human brain? Is it something that we have to be taught as children? Do we need role models for it? Does it occur in non-human animals, also? Etcetera.

While all these theoretical enquiries may play a part on the level of ego-based storytelling in the relative world, they do not take into consideration even the existence of true nature, let alone its influence, and thus remain oblivious to the Blindspot. Which renders all such explorations only partial. Because true nature is itself the essence of altruistic, the essence of kind. It is kindness through and through, and knows nothing contrary to that. In fact, it's so very kind that it is beyond the opposite of itself.

---

* Claim made by world-class romantic sentimentalist, yours truly.

X

MEDIATED

The mind, poor thing, must do what it does.* As the pre-eminent instrument of duality—indeed the instrument through which the entire edifice of subject/object, space/time is constructed and maintained—it will take even the most profound, ecstatic, nondual experiences of truth (including those encountered in near-death occurrences), and convert them into, well, an *it*. How could it not?

So... anybody who comes to realize truth will, by necessity, have to describe it in terms limited to what can be conceived, and usually this will be colored by her own particular background. The Christian, for example, steeped in her culture and tradition, will "come back" from any such ecstatic immersion speaking of Christ and Holy Spirit and Grace. The Buddhist will testify about emptiness. The Sufi will cry about the Beloved.

None of which is a problem...until we, their audience, start to *believe* them, instantly translating their descriptions into prescriptions. Not until we take their language and immediately convert it into recipes we can latch on to, make sense of, cling to, for the comfort of certainty. That's what mind does, after all. How could it do otherwise? When we start believing our own or others' descriptions *about* truth, we are simply trying to corral the naked, unutterable freefall of realization into something familiar to us. Something that can be understood. Which is understandable.

* In most contemplative spiritual circles (other than Buddhist), the word "mind" is considered to be interchangeable with the concepts of "ego" or "conditioned self," as distinct from "consciousness" or "true nature," which is unconditioned.

We can't think in any other way. Our entire conceptual apparatus is built upon objective representations. You may think you're reading a book right now, for example. But you're not; you're reading a "book." The thing itself, whatever you call it or don't call it, remains forever out of your field of conceptual knowingness. As soon as we learn to attach a label to things—and it's always a learned behavior—we cease to see them as they are in their bare actualities. What we see instead are their representations in our minds, and as we've noted, this is especially so when it comes to our "selves."

No less especially, when it comes to God. What's often forgotten is that all spiritual teachings, even the highest, are merely pointers to the truth—not the thing itself. Because (remember), there *is* no such "thing." The famous Zen metaphor cautions us not to take the finger pointing at the moon for the moon itself. But it's less often warned that even the moon itself is *also* not the moon.

When we believe our own conceptual constructions about God, we are actually flouting the First Commandment. For then, we are indeed guilty of "placing other gods before Me," the gods of virtual representation.* As theologian Paul Tillich put it: "[The] idea that the human mind is a perpetual manufacturer of idols is one of the deepest things which can be said about our thinking of God."[23]

And as the 13th-century Dominican monk Meister Eckhart pleaded, "God, please relieve me of 'God'!"

To stretch a term coined by anthropologist Thomas De Zengotita, what we are describing here is the process of "mediation." It is through this relentless mechanism of representational imaging—if we are suckered into believing it—that we estrange ourselves from truth. We are banished from the Garden just by dint of being born with minds, which is precisely how the teaching of original sin might well be interpreted from an esoteric perspective. But wait—it gets worse, much worse.

---

* Although we're doing it quite innocently; it's not a sin.

As if the mediating mechanism of mind alone wasn't bad enough, we now live in a culture where its effects on us get magnified many times over by...the media. This is Thomas De Zengotita's argument (as amplified by yours truly). Namely: If the mind itself is the primal mediating filter of all experience, then this mechanism gets exponentially magnified by the images and messages assaulting us from every direction by the ubiquitous intrusions of modern communications technology.

"Ask yourself," De Zengotita prods, "is there anything you do that remains essentially unmediated, anything you don't experience reflexively through some commodified representation of it?"[24]

Yes, just try to think of even one area of your life in which some image from advertising or the movies or the news or the magazines or the Web...has not sneakily interposed itself between you and your actual experience. It's an image you may not even know you're harboring, until in some private moment it creeps into awareness—and not infrequently, in this postmodern age, with some tinge of irony. Reading a "bedtime story" to your child? Having "a talk" with your teenager? "Watching your diet"? Becoming a "loser"? Or a "winner?" Having an affair with "someone at the office"? Notice all those quotation marks; that's a tip-off that some mediating effect is at work. It's as if you can't even think anymore outside the hectoring echo of the headlines and the captions and the pesky memes. Working up some feelings for the "earthquake victims" in Turkey? "Throwing yourself into the arms" of your fiancé, fresh back from deployment?

Yes, even in your most intimate moments: You're in passionate embrace with your beloved, and you open your mouth against his... *just-so*. How would you have known which angle of head, what precise parting of lips, what position of tongue...had it not been for the hundreds of Hollywood images you've got stored up, seeping like oil into the scene? Hell, a person can't even masturbate anymore without some handed-down image intruding into the act. Admit it.*

Really now: How do you know when to give a standing ovation after a performance? When to "douse the coach" with Gatorade after a team victory? When to "applaud the drummer" when he goes to his cymbals during his solo? (Hint: we've all learned the consensual cues, haven't we?; and we reflexively follow them, whether or not the solo was any good.)

It may be subtle, but a little reflection will reveal the degree to which this media-mediating mechanism saturates our experience with its invisible, all-pervasive insidiousness. It's so clever that it can even appear to let us in on the joke, as if we were insiders to the very representations we're being fed, as if they're saying to us, "Aren't we all so smart? Aren't we all so hip and sophisticated?"

I think the first moment in movies when I became aware of this mechanism was the famous scene in the first Indiana Jones film, when Harrison Ford, confronted by a fierce, swaggering, bare-chested, sword-twirling foe, lets his face shift from horrified dismay to a what-the-hell smirk, before blowing the guy away with his pistol. That look was aimed at us, in the audience, and we knew it. And dug it.

As we dig it now, too, more than ever. See any television commentary by a clever late-host host; watch any current rom-com movie. We are all so cunning, colluding together in our own ironic distancing from ourselves.

I'm reminded of the story told by a famous rock band groupie who had slept with dozens of rock stars. Every time she slept with some new rock star, she'd tell her friends, "He was great, but he wasn't any Mick Jagger." Eventually, though, she did finally bag Mick Jagger, himself, in the flesh. When asked to give her review, she said: "He was *great*—but he wasn't any Mick Jagger."

---

* I do wonder how people kissed before there were movies. Maybe they didn't?

From a different direction, allow me to share one example from my own personal history. Growing up in Maine in the halcyon 1950s, I somehow became drawn to wild nature, and spent every moment I could tramping off into the hills of my state and into neighboring New Hampshire. Who knows where this allure came from? Certainly not from my parents, nor from the prevailing Downeastern culture, either, which was steeped in hunting and fishing. Few people had ever heard of just tramping around the woods, appreciating them, absorbing them...communing with them and the creatures that lived therein.

My experience in nature as a youngster was filled with mystery, hardship, sweetness, comfort, sweatiness, freezing-my-ass-off-ness, tormenting bugginess, hunger, thirst, fright, awe...wonder. Even now, it still can be. But in the meantime I have absorbed so many thousands of images of happy, sexy, Gore-Tex-clad couples clambering up mountainsides...virile, sunburnt extreme-mountaineers kicking steps with their becramponed, yellow plastic boots into gleaming snowslopes above the clouds...laughing bronzed lovelies all in lilac Lycra, paddling kayaks through pods of smiling dolphins...stunning telephoto slow-mo close-ups of leaping cougars and breaching whales and loping packs of wolves....

...that even someone as supposedly sensitive as I (?) has had his psyche infiltrated. Something cunning has appropriated the rawness of a direct relationship with nature, its essential strangeness and unfathomableness. When I am lucky enough to spot a bear in the woods these days, just dozing in the sun, it's hard (I confess) not to wish that it would get up and *do* something, already. The unadorned tree-hugging behavior that to the old-time Mainers seemed odd and suspect has now become hip and fashionable. It has been made into an industry, a product, just another pastime—one among so many other choices—dressed up and glamorized to sell to what De Zengotita calls the "flattered self."

The word that mountaineering guide Jack Turner uses to describe an encounter with nature such as the kind I experienced in childhood is "aura." Any natural wonder that is encountered freshly and rawly communicates a mystery that is liable to send chills down one's spine and currents of delight up one's heart: such is that place's or phenomenon's *aura*. But that initial encounter cannot be repeated in any future visit, if one holds any agenda about it, any expectation of a repeat performance. *Aura* is a delicate thing. And it is destroyed not only by any conceptual agendas, but also by reviewing photos, taking photos, perusing social media postings, making social media postings, reading guidebooks about such places or phenomena, writing guidebooks about the same....

The layering of images, factual knowledge, and interpretations over the raw, immediate impact of a natural place, animal, or phenomenon—or work of art, for that matter—renders its aura void. As Turner says, "Indeed, the three together—knowledge [of the guidebook kind]... photography [of the social media kind], and mass tourism [of the packaged pampered kind] are the unholy trinity that destroys the mysteries of both art and nature."[25] And as an explorer and expedition guide into wild places all over the world, he is someone who should know.

Although it doesn't require an expert. Take a look at the average tourist who stops his car at some scenic lookout point in any given national park. Observe his behavior; what does he do when confronted by such an...um, "awesome" piece of "scenery"? Hint: What's that gizmo he clutches in his hand? Where does he herd the wife and kids in order to get a better "shot"? How does he behave after he has "saved the memory" and can't think of anything else...to *do*? How long does he linger?

Leaving the mountains for a moment: The Mona Lisa, after years of enduring forests of upstretched arms clutching cellphones, finally had to place a ban on all photo-taking in her section of the Louvre (or at least the management did). The tourists complained bitterly. How else, after all, would they ever be able to capture her forever, for their very own?*

* I will restrain myself from describing the behavior of phone-bearing tourists at...Auschwitz.

At a different museum, in Berlin, the famous painting by Rembrandt, *The Man with the Golden Helmet*, used to attract such huge crowds that people were urged to move along so that others behind could get their view...until it was determined in 1985 that the masterpiece was not actually painted by Rembrandt after all, but by someone else. Someone unknown. And after that, the crowds just passed *The Man* on by, giving him scarcely a glance. Same magnificent painting, same mysterious image, same gallery. . .just not carrying that vaunted label, so who cared?

Or how about this story told by George Clooney: There he was, on a red carpet surrounded by crowds of jostling fans. So, being the nice guy that he is, he extends his hand over the barrier rope to shake hands with a smiling woman—and meets only her clutched phone. Better the screened image than the actual Clooney flesh, it seems.

Back to nature: Take a look at the average guided raft float down a section of wild river. See the happy urbanites in their orange life-vests getting their amusement park-like thrills in the sun and spray. (Jack Turner calls such folks "fun hogs.") Does it ever cross their minds (or guts) that they're immersed in a vast interplay of inconceivable forces utterly indifferent to their personal existences? Are they ever *stunned silent* by this?*

But here's the rub: This trend is not altogether without merit. I can testify, myself, that Gore-Tex and goose down are far more comfortable than those scratchy old woolen Mackintoshes, possibly even lifesaving. And they look so much sharper as well; who can argue with that? My lightweight aluminum snowshoes with bright blue plastic webbing and instant bindings have it all over my damned old heavy wooden contraptions, notwithstanding any residual soft spot I might harbor for their old-timey esthetics.

---

* Newsflash (2014): rangers in our national forests have had to post signs warning visitors not to take selfies with...bears.

Moreover, as Susan Sontag famously complained, "Nature has no sense of irony." And the deal is, I *like* irony. I like my bears galumphing. I would probably enjoy Sunday river-raft floats, if I ever did one. I like seeing other people's vacation photos (although I do not take any, myself). I like my political commentary smart. I like Judd Apatow rom-coms, too.

So once again, none of this mediating stuff is necessarily a problem. When it comes to truth, the game is always about *seeing through* the pageantries of phenomena, rather than resisting them. As long as you know that the real light shines outside the entrance, there's nothing wrong about enjoying the shadowplay on the walls of Plato's cave. The only relevant question is: Where are you *rooted*—in the light or the shadows? If you still take the shadows to be reality, then you will tend to be the unconscious fodder for the agencies of mediation, which have their own agendas.

Neurobiologists tell us that the self has its fundamental origins in the single brain cell, the neuron. But the neuron itself can only fire or not fire, it shows up on an fMRI as either lit up or not—hardly anything that can explain the sense of a unified, subjective *me*. So maybe it's an effect of zillions of neurons firing in certain coordinated ways, over certain specialized circuits, that accounts for this ongoing sense of a self, propose the neuroscientists. Maybe this coordinated orchestration is the way that the mind uses the brain to make sense of the chaotic torrent of incoming data, memory, experience, sensation, perception. It seeks some kind of coherence amidst all those neural firings, some kind of central management. That's the mind's job, after all; its service to the survival of the organism.

And it does the job well: from out of the noise of neural chaos it weaves the cohesiveness of narrative. The mind's coordinated neural orchestration, in other words, can be described as something like a story the brain is telling itself. And its most fundamental story is that it has, or rather *is*, a self.

Which happens to be in alignment with what the nondual sages have been telling us all along: that the self is nothing more than a story we keep telling ourselves in every moment. A fictitious sense of authorship. A tapestry in imagination, sometimes happy, sometimes sad, but always made-up. In other words, and more to the point: it's a *mediation*. It is, in fact, the primal mediation. This is not to say that there is nothing underlying that tapestry that's actually true—a true identity or true nature—but this is where the neuroscientists come screeching to a halt. Such notions are just not part of their vocabulary, yet one more mark of the Blindspot.

But for the esoteric spiritual seeker, for whom "true nature" is a catchphrase of everyday speech, all of this stuff about "story" constitutes a predicament; and it would seem that such a one may be faced with a few more challenges around it today than ever before. I mean, first we human primates had to deal with (and enjoy) the mediating effects of symbolic language, which was a huge evolutionary leap. And then we had to deal with (and enjoy) the mediating effects of literacy—which hasn't been easy, to say the least. For both of these bio-cultural advances have led to a massive strengthening in our neural storytelling powers, and have thereby only solidified the cohesiveness of our imagined selves, our conviction of a separate, decision-making *me*.

For all their undeniable benefits, in other words, each stage of human evolution has only strengthened the play of abstraction and virtuality, adding one more layer between us and reality. But wait: today we have to deal with this massive, omnipresent, infiltrating, representational effect of the technological media as well!

Could it get any worse?

Maybe. For now, the mediating effect extends even to such qualities as compassion and love and forgiveness. Indeed to spirituality, itself. Concepts like "All is One" and "Love is All" and "We Are the World"—there's *nothing* that the mind, with great assistance from today's media, cannot get its storytelling hands on. How many paradigm-challenging movies do we need to watch about shifts in consciousness and quantum leaps and new awakenings, and *What the Bleep?*, before the hi-def images emblazoned in our neurons completely overwhelm any possibility of the *actualities* they portray becoming realized by us, unproduced and unexpected, first-hand? How many *Avatar*(s) do we need to watch, before we start to believe that "union with nature" is no different than Union with Nature? How many HD Smart TV close-ups showing aid workers-without-borders caring for wounded toddlers do we need to watch, before we can no longer tell the difference between "compassion" and Compassion? How many friends do we need to make on Facebook before we no longer know who our friends are?

And: cue the music. Notice the swelling violins whenever any image of "spiritual feeling" appears on the movie screen. Notice how the cellos modulate upward as the devotee raises her arms, creases her brows, and closes her eyes (and it is always a her). Notice the trumpets rising to climax as the shafts of sunlight burst down from the skies, through the boughs of the redwoods, illuminating the supplicant's upturned face, as she folds her hands over her heart.

Please: gag me with a spoon.*

And now, for the *coup de grace*: Double-Rainbow Guy. Perhaps forgotten by the time you read this, DRG refers to a video that went viral on YouTube in July 2010. The visual portion of this offering shows a double rainbow, arching through the skies over a mountain near Yosemite, California. Nice, even if a little boring after ten minutes of low-res, handheld-wiggling image of a nearly static view. But it's the

* Mediated curse intentional, if outdated.

audio portion that grabs you. It's nothing less than the eavesdropping on a man in the grips of orgasmic ecstasy. Yes, he's moaning and groaning and shouting, helplessly, over and over: "OH, OHH, OH MY GOD!!!!" "IT'S A DOUBLE-RAINBOW, ALL THE WAY!" "OHH-OHHH! IT'S SO INTENSE!!" Over and over and over. And, "OH MY GOD, IT'S *ALL THE WAY*...WHAT COULD THIS *MEAN*?!?" On and on, like that. It's a portrait of a man who has let go of all propriety, in complete thrall to the essential mystery of existence.

Or is it?

Maybe I'm betraying a generational gap here, but why did this guy find it necessary to introduce the smartphone screen into his experience, in the first place? Why did he need to hold the camera up before his eyes, the whole ecstatic time? What is this about, this new compulsion to record and post every detail of our lives today, no matter how intensely intimate? No matter how "spiritual"?

Sure, you could say that Double-Rainbow Guy just wanted to share such a joyful experience with others, that he was motivated by a kind of innocent exuberance. And I think there may be some truth to that. From what I could tell, the guy had a genuinely warm, childlike spirit. I'm not poo-pooing his impulse, entirely.

But here's what's happened, as of this writing: The video has been viewed 50,000,000 times on YouTube. Double-Rainbow Guy himself has appeared on national television (*Jimmy Kimmel Live*). The story was picked up by all the major networks, which ran stories on it. The event has been celebrated in a widely played pop song, employing such lyrics as "It's *all the way!* It's *so intense!*" And when people watch the video (as the studio audience did during the Kimmel taping) or hear the song, the universal response they have is: laughter.

Well, me too. I laughed out loud; couldn't help it. But I also find this curious. I mean, what are we all laughing *at*?

It's as if we're a bit mortified by the guy's unrehearsed, immodest behavior. We let out a reflexive, self-conscious titter about a display that's so Dionysian, so immoderate, so...*lacking restraint*, in a certain way. Or, more to the point: We're embarrassed by how instantly and deeply we *resonate* with such behavior. Yes, as long as we keep that screen up in front of our eyes, as long as we can click on the image, whistle the tune, we can retain our distance, our sense of control. But deep down, a part of us knows better; the Blindspot hovers just off-frame. We can watch the DRG video in apparent safety and appreciate the childlike exuberance on display; we can "relate" to it, even. But we know how thin the veiling screen really is. And we laugh in defensive discomfiture over our felt vulnerability.

But there is a slight cost here: After watching the Double Rainbow Guy video, how many of us will ever be able to encounter an actual double rainbow unarmed, unprepared and naked ever again? Where will its aura have gone? How many of us will ever be able to see such a thing in the mountain sky after a summer rainstorm and not have an instant laugh-track spring to our inner ears?

Ahh, mediated again.

Seeing through mediated displays means to see, to really *get*, that the difference between "Oh my God" as pop song lyric and "*Oh my God!*" as the terror of self-annihilation, is categorical. It means to really *get* that the answer to "What could this mean?" is nothing less than silence. It means to get that Love exists in a completely different dimension than does "love." That wilderness as playground has nothing in common with wilderness as sanctuary. That there is absolutely no continuity between "compassion" and Compassion, as it is, itself. The (no)Thing, Itself.

Yet it's so easy to get fooled, so very easy. Our culturally reinforced, sentimental buttons sucker us, every time. And it's only going to get worse, as the almighty techno-gadget, both handheld and wall-sized, intervenes in—screens—every aspect of our lives. And I mean *every* aspect...*from* every aspect.[*] So it comes down to what we really want. If we want the truth, then we must awaken to the open secret in the Blindspot. For an unknown frontier separates "compassion" from Compassion, "surrender" from Surrender, "silence" from Silence. Like the winking pseudo-orbits of electrons, the space betwixt is discontinuous.

I am not suggesting that double-rainbow guys should stop posting videos or that aid workers in Haiti should hide from the camera. Or even that we stop watching any of them do what they do on our iPads. Just that we become clear that the one thing (the mediational image) does not lead to the other (the unknowable mystery that it *is*). A quality referred to in quotes does not help anyone realize that which it represents. The mind's conception of something actually conceals what that something *is*, its essential *beingness*. Its *aura*.

Even so, this is not a matter of right or wrong. To live a mediated existence is not evil, as such. Yet there is something inherently twisted in the proposition that an all-senses virtual display of a mortar attack in Ukraine will *lessen* the viewer's sense of personal distance from the actuality of such world events. For there is a price to be paid in a mediated existence—a life once-removed (or more) from the real thing. A life lived in a representation, a kind of amnesia, forgetful that that's all it is.

It's a life in which we've forgotten that we're only pretending that the naked king is all dressed up in his finery. A life in which we are trapped in the *Matrix*, having forgotten that we did it to ourselves and could undo it at any time. A life in which we have abstracted ourselves from ourselves, others, and God. A life in which we continue to live in the flickering shadowplay of mind, a virtual reality even *before* any other representations are stacked up upon it. A life guaranteed to perpetuate the subjective sense of wanting more. Wanting, actually, *less*: the real, actual, un-abstracted thing. Wanting, finally...the end of wanting.

---

* Frosting on this toxic cake: virtual and augmented reality devices; also personal video filters. Virtuality superimposed upon virtuality superimposed upon virtuality... Just what we need.

XI

BRIDGING THE GAP

If you should happen to get into a religious discussion with a typical postmodern person (not recommended) and reveal to her that you have a "spiritual teacher," and that you belong to a small community that has gathered around him or her to explore the deep understandings described so far, it will simply not register with her. Ditto if you tell her that you travel to Peru twice a year to take ayahuasca with your shaman. Or that you maintain a daily practice of meditation, guided by your (Hindu) guru.* Or that you maintain a daily (Christian) practice of Centering Prayer, guided by your innovative priest. Let alone if you say, "My religion goes by the name 'nonduality' or 'hesychasm' or '*Advaita*,' if it needs to be called anything at all."

When not met with stares of incomprehension, such declarations usually trigger the reflexive conclusions about cults or *woo-woo*, expressed or not. Confessions such as "I'm a Buddhist" or "I practice yoga"—both venerable gateway vehicles—do elicit higher levels of name-recognition, yet it's amazing how much corruption even such familiar labels have suffered, when trickled down through the common media gauze. It doesn't take much discrimination to see how distorted the term "zen" has become in popular usage today, in everything from advertising copy ("the zen of car shopping") to health products ("Zentoes"), to common speech ("it's all so very zen"). And where yoga has been reduced to a form of weight control and stress relief. And where—oh, I can't even begin to broach what's been wreaked on the term "tantric."

---

* Although these last two activities are fast becoming mediated as "dope" by mainstream culture.

Be that as it may, a number of encouraging trends have emerged in recent years in the arts and sciences that seek to penetrate the Blindspot in their own ways. Many of these trends owe their inspiration to the discoveries in quantum physics, whose implications regarding this thing called consciousness cannot be ignored, even though many physicists persist in trying. We will dive headlong into those implications in the next few chapters.

"Consciousness Studies" is the umbrella term for a field enjoying popularity on college campuses and sprouting its own network of multidisciplinary conferences and publications. Under this rubric, moreover, a slew of new theories and sub-specialties have sprung up in recent years that each take a slightly different angle on the subject. Whether it be Donald Hoffman with his "multimodal user interface" theory or Deepak Chopra with his "qualia science" or David Bohm with his model of "implicate and explicate orders" or Penrose and Hameroff with their "Orch-OR Theory" or Menas Kafatos with his "Amazing Hypothesis"...they are all chipping away at the same non-dual One (no)Thing, but just coming at it from more typically scientific backgrounds and coming up with different terminologies. Doing their bit to bridge the gap and penetrate the Blindspot.

Even within the broad canopy of consciousness studies, however, the Blindspot often finds a way of persisting. It's difficult for academicians to wrap their heads around the understanding that consciousness can refer to something not exclusively personal to an individual human being. That it might more accurately refer to That in which all subjective experience arises *within* (and also *as*). When students of consciousness studies study consciousness, what many of them actually examine is the experience of subjective mind and not consciousness itself, which is *prior* to anybody's mind, no matter how personally subjective the experience of it may feel.

So it's encouraging to find a few folks coming at it from both directions, with their feet in both the scientific world and the mystical/direct-experiential world. Believe it or not, it's quite possible to awaken to reality, even if you happen to have a natural predisposition toward academic scholarship. Knowing that I will inevitably leave out dozens of worthy 20th- and 21st-century candidates, I hesitate to name names; but all the same I can't resist listing the ubiquitous Deepak Chopra, Eckhart Tolle, A.H. Almaas, Joseph Chilton Pearce, and Ken Wilber, just to give you some idea of what I'm talking about. Okay, I might also add Amit Goswami, Jean Klein, Francis Lucille, Franklin Merrell-Wolff, Joseph Campbell, Matthieu Ricard, Brian Swimme, Michael Spezio, Donald Hoffman, Mauro Zappaterra, Peter Russell... True, not all of them are still alive, but all are contemporary enough for me to dub them "bridging personalities."

Even as major a scientific dude as Max Planck, the originator of quantum theory, said in 1931:

> I regard consciousness as fundamental. I regard matter as derivative from consciousness. We cannot get behind consciousness. Everything that we talk about, everything that we regard as existing, postulates consciousness.[26]

And I haven't even mentioned an entirely different category of potential bridging personality—the figures who have emerged from the exoteric religious camp in the last century, willing to even defy their "superiors" when necessary, in order to disseminate their own profound esoteric discoveries to a wider public. I refer to such people as Thomas Merton, Bernadette Roberts, David Cooper, Shlomo Carlebach, Tessa Bielecki, Cynthia Bourgeault, Thomas Keating, Karen Armstrong, Thomas Berry and Regina Sara Ryan, to name just a few.*

Even a few Hollywood personalities are starting to play a bridging role these days—Jim Carrey, Alan Arkin (sadly deceased), Alan Ball, and Terrence Malick come to mind.

---

* Apologies to everyone I've left out.

Thus, the Blindspot that is the focus of this book may be fraying somewhat at the edges of the culture. There are definite signs that attention is being directed toward some promising places. As to where it all may lead, well...we shall see.

Nevertheless, no discussion of bridging personalities would be complete without mentioning the contribution of the great American psychologist/philosopher William James, whose 1902 classic, *The Varieties of Religious Experience*, was an attempt to lend scientific credibility to all kinds of non-ordinary subjective happenings. In that book, James argued that these mystical experiences deserved a more elevated status in our reckoning than they usually receive. I repeat here what is probably his most quoted passage:

> It is that our normal waking consciousness, rational consciousness as we call it, is but one special type of consciousness, whilst all about it, parted from it by the filmiest of screens, there lie potential forms of consciousness entirely different. We may go through life unsuspecting their existence; but apply the requisite stimulus, and at a touch they are there in all their completeness... No account of the universe in its totality can be final which leaves these other forms of consciousness quite disregarded. ....They forbid a premature closing of our accounts with reality.[27]

Now, James was talking only about mystical experiences, not nondual awakening, and these are not the same thing.* This is a feature of

* A slight refinement: Mystical experiences can be nondual awakenings. However, because they are almost always transient, they are usually interpreted through the limited filter determined by the person's everyday stage of spiritual maturity.

the Blindspot that comes up again and again: Awakening is *not* an experience, per se, and the idea that it *is* some kind of experience (of the extraordinary kind) is a common misperception that arises frequently, wherever things spiritual are discussed. Sure, in retrospect, once her mind kicks back in, the person who has awakened may assign an experiential wording to it, just to be able to talk about whatever happened to her. But any experience that might have accompanied the event was itself not the point, only a by-product. "Enlightenment is not *an* experience," to quote Rupert Spira, "it is the revelation of the true nature of *all* experience." Any experience, no matter how mind-blowing, implies that old dualistic relationship between the experiencer and that which is experienced. Whereas, in nondual awakening, that duality collapses. Collapses into *what*?

Just This. Or in other words:

[silence]

Do I repeat myself? Yet it's worth repeating, especially in this section, which is all about the potentially blindspotting snare of experience. As said Wittgenstein, "Whereof one cannot speak, thereof one must be silent." And Rumi, too: "Silence is the language of God. All else is poor translation."

Still, translatable experiences can have their value. The non-ordinary experiences catalogued by James may not be ultimate, but they are often the first inklings that people may have, that there is something more available out there in the ineffable vastness of existence. They represent a foreshadowing, a clue, which may often be enough to start someone down the esoteric spiritual path, straight into the Tiger's Jaws.

Which naturally leads us to a brief consideration of drugs.* Particularly the psychedelic kind, such as LSD, psilocybin, DMT, peyote, MDMA, and, yes, even modest marijuana. In their ability to induce vivid and powerful mystical experiences, these substances have served as bridges for more than one unsuspecting person over the years. So it's really no wonder that such substances are so instantly rendered illegal and anathema by all upstanding, God-fearing, God-denying, God-whatever governments all over the world. For it is precisely this "premature closing of our accounts with reality" that modern societies strive to maintain above all else—lest the job of governing whole populations become unmanageable.

I'm not the first one to argue the futility of the war on drugs. But it's less often observed how this issue reflects all the confusions and ambivalences the culture holds about esotericism in general, all the ambivalences being played out in our collective psyches: Our nervous, jokey fascination with drugs, even while we outlaw them. Just say the syllables, L-S-D—and notice the secret *frisson* it triggers in you, maybe even a self-conscious titter, even as we lock users away and prohibit clinical research on the substance.† Similarly, the word "weed" (in contrast to the legalized/sanitized/Latinized term "cannabis").

It is no accident that modern societies make legal and social exceptions regarding the one drug, alcohol, that is probably the *least* effective for triggering the kinds of experiences that might serve as bridging ones (and *most* effective for keeping the Blindspot what it already is).‡

---

* As it did William James.

† In a recent *New Yorker* review, the writer asserted that the impulse to even ask the Big Questions of life was usually relegated only to "people who have gravely misjudged their tolerance for edibles." Titter away: the sting of truthiness.

‡ Note the additional bridging personalities Lenny Bruce, George Carlin, and Cheech & Chong—who attempted to bring these cultural ambivalences out of the closet.

This is not to suggest that drug use is in any way necessary for the realization of truth. It most certainly is not. Yet our broader cultural attitudes toward such substances are instructive as reflections of each person's inner relationship with the truth that is so effectively hidden in the Blindspot:

We want the truth, yet we fear it.

We find ourselves craning towards it, fascinated by it, yet then we draw back, afraid we'll lose our grip on whatever security we're holding onto.

We yearn for truth, sure, yet deep down we know what price we will ultimately need to pay—namely, our "selves," as we have imagined ourselves to be.

Although most of us nowadays do a good job of distracting ourselves with all manner of pressing concerns and beguiling entertainments, there is something deep inside us that knows that true liberation—freedom, happiness, peace—lies in a stripping away of all that stuff, especially the stuff that makes us imagine that our constructed selves are who we are. And although this stripping process is decidedly *not* a project of self-abnegation or asceticism or self-flagellation or ultra-fasting or righteous celibacy—all of which only end up reinforcing the very self that seeks its own penetration—the process does remain a humbling one. It does require an attitude of the deepest humility, in which we may ultimately stand naked in the face of the cosmos—or God, if you will. Such is the meekness spoken of by Jesus. A scary prospect, to be sure.*

What this stripping process does require is exquisitely tuned to each individual and thus takes eight billion different forms, well beyond the scope of this book. The constructed self's fear of this process is both well-founded and illusory. It is justified because this self knows

---

* The most common cause of psychedelic "bad trips" is the person's inability or unwillingness to surrender without resistance to all the emotional states, visual images, and auditory assaults that can occur for him.

that, taken to its culmination, the process will indeed topple it from its usurped throne as king or queen of its realm. But the truth of the matter is that nothing real is lost, only that which had little reality to begin with. So the fear is not justified at all, and even the word "stripping" is not entirely warranted.

But a person cannot know this ahead of time, and that's the rub. It becomes evident only once the process has reached a critical mass. Until such time, to imagine any such process can remain a terrifying prospect.

So finally we shrink away, most of us, anyway. And we take up residence on the familiar, exoteric side of the gap in our worldviews and beliefs. Alan Watts* blamed this habitual reflex on "the taboo against knowing who you are," which he saw running so rampant in this culture[28]—his way of describing the same Blindspot that is the subject of this book. Think of all the blood spilt and money spent in the noble fight against drugs, in defense of that taboo, this undivine Blindspot!

Yes, back to the bridging role of drugs, specifically of the psychedelic variety.† Again, I'm not suggesting that any experience of expanded consciousness is the same thing as realizing truth. They're not. And certainly, the use of drugs to achieve that expansion carries substantial risks, especially in a society that lacks initiated elders. It's just that such altered states, when properly guided, *can* help in the cultivation of esoteric curiosity. The gut experience of them can loosen our firmly held convictions and persuade us that reality may not be as real as we had assumed. And the light of truth does shine brighter, when given the invitation that such curiosity extends toward it. The veil does get thinner, even unto death itself.‡ The roadsigns say: THIS WAY.

---

* The late, influential teacher whose use of certain helpful substances was not unknown—and who makes a disembodied appearance in the 2013 movie, *Her*.

† Which are currently called "entheogens," literally meaning "generating god within."

‡ And maybe beyond, as Leary, Alpert and Metzger so lucidly hypothesized in their 1964 classic, *The Psychedelic Experience*.[29]

And just perhaps, that's *really* why we've made LSD illegal. This war on drugs may end up costing us even more than we suspect.

Something interesting is occurring on the bleeding edge of physics and philosophy these days. Since what we call physical reality has become increasingly hard to pin down, or even adequately classify, "one begins to wonder," states theologian Philip Clayton, "whether there is something fundamentally flawed in the idea of a world built up out of matter."

As we'll see in the next chapter, this assertion is not even considered fringe or marginal anymore by a growing coterie of scientists. "It appears that, each time the greatest systematic philosophers have attempted to define [matter]," says Clayton, "it has receded again and again from their grasp."[30]

But if we cannot place matter at the bottom, the foundation, of our conceptual underpinning for the universe, what *can* we use? Among these contemporary thinkers the answer is *information*. Seriously. The study of Information as the foundational building block of the universe has become a thriving subspecialty for a growing community of physicists, biologists, philosophers and theologians. Simply, this new conceptual hierarchy posits information at the bottom, out of which emerges the laws of physics, out of which emerges (finally) matter (whatever that is).

And from there, of course, emerges all the conjurations of physics itself. And from that, all chemical phenomena. And from that, all biological phenomena. And from that, all processes psychological. And here we are.

The gist of this theoretical terrain is the intuition that there must be something even prior to the laws of physics, something that lends it an animating "aboutness"—something that promotes the "merely possible" to the "actually existing." It's the something that inaugurates the cipher of all possible universes and all possible genomes. A source code, if you will. As no less a thinker than Stephen Hawking has put it:

> The usual approach of science to construct a mathematical model cannot answer the question of why there should be a universe for the model to describe. Why does the universe go through all the trouble of existing?[31]

And along the same wavelength, physicist Paul Davies expands on this theme and further tracks down this elusive concept of *aboutness*:

> Given that the universe could be otherwise, in vastly many different ways, what is it that determines the way the universe actually is? Expressed differently, given the apparently limitless number of entities that can exist, who or what gets to decide what *actually* exists? The universe contains certain things: stars, planets, atoms, living organisms... Why do *those* things exist rather than others? Why not pulsating green jelly, or interwoven chains, or fractal hyperspheres? The same issue arises for the laws of physics. Why does gravity obey an inverse square law rather than an inverse cubed law? Why are there two varieties of electric charge rather than four, and three "flavors" of neutrino rather than seven? Even if we had a unified theory that connected all these facts, we would still be left with the puzzle of why *that* theory is "the chosen one."

Davies then quotes Hawking to place the cherry on top:

> What is it that breathes fire into the equations and makes a universe for them to describe? [32]

Sound familiar, at least flavorwise? It may be because this postmodern academic approach to the mysteries of existence possesses a lot in common with the ancient nondual perspective, at least conceptually. And although it bears repeating that nonduality as a conceptual philosophy is not equivalent to nondual realization as a lived experience (in and as this selfsame bodymind, right now)...still, Information Theory (as it's called) could develop into a useful bridging discipline, and its proponents into true bridging personalities. As physicist A.K. Mukhopadhyay puts it, "Information could be the bridging link between the two titans, local science of time, space, energy, and matter and nonlocal science of consciousness, mind, self, and life-principle."[28]

In any case, these information theorists are asking the right questions, conducting enquiries that any nondual sage would recognize as useful. Here in this new discipline the link between the exoteric and esoteric worlds is being built—as well as between science and religion. "The time has come," states Mukhopadhyay, "when information needs to be looked at as an independent agency connecting the physical and the non-physical realms."[29]

One last bridging plank: the Science and Nonduality (SAND) community (see *scienceandnonduality.com*), where notable representatives from both the scientific and the nondual worlds—including many whose names I've dropped in this text—come together and compare notes on these two distinct ways of approaching the same (no)Thing. As I've mentioned before, there do exist a few progressive islands out there, where these ideas are not quite so foreign. May they continue to multiply over the globe, for the benefit of all beings!

As fine a hair as this may be, there may be something even prior to information (depending upon how one defines that term). From the nondual perspective, the foundational ground of the universe from which information and *aboutness* and the laws of physics and then eventually what we call "matter" are all piggybacked upon and within, is nothing other than that One (no)Thing we have been talking about all along. Rather than information, we could call it Pure Intelligence (or Omniscience).

Yet the term consciousness (or "awaring presence") may be even better, as it is a term that can be related to in a personal way. For whatever that (no)Thing is, it is the true nature of your own, intimate self. It is the reason why that which is looking out of your eyes right now is the same as that which was looking out of your eyes when you were five years old. Or twenty. You may have noticed this from time to time—how, from the inside, you somehow don't feel any older now than you ever did, no matter how you appear in the bathroom mirror. Something that you know must be "you" in some indescribable way… never grows old!

In fact, the first experience you ever had as a newborn baby was experienced by this same Whatever that is looking out of your eyes right now. It was magically present when you were born…and yet you never experienced *its* appearance. It was already there, because whatever this ineffable (no)Thing is, it never comes and goes. It will never even go anywhere after you die.

And not so incidentally, whatever this unthingy thing is, it's identical to that which is looking out of *my* eyes. And the eyes of every living being in the universe (and nonliving beings as well, in whatever unknowable form their "eyes" might take).

XII

SIX BLIND SPOTS, PART 1

Disclaimer: I am aware of all the wide-eyed attempts made in recent years, through popular books and films, at using the discoveries of quantum physics in the last hundred years to prove or confirm the claims of mystics and spiritual adepts throughout the millennia. I am aware of how such books and movies make many actual physicists want to hide beneath their desks out of sheer embarrassment.

I get it. Distortions have certainly been made. Claims have often been nothing more than wishful, to put the most charitable spin on it. I am therefore quite aware that I walk on eggshells to say another word on the subject.

Yet I would also feel grossly negligent if I didn't at least try. For although some scientists may cringe at the thought of their work being associated with spirituality of any sort, many more have just mistakenly conflated all spirituality with mysticism—and the latter term is fraught with way too much baggage for them. They therefore shy away with a vengeance from its taint, with all of its 19th century parlor-game connotations. As they should (up to a point).

But many scientists also suffer from a disease called FAPP.

Of the many remarkable features of quantum mechanics, one of them is that when theory-neutral experiments are performed, they are always proven correct. Indeed, they are *never* proven wrong. It's only when quantum *theory* raises its weirdling head that things simply get too uncomfortable for many classically-trained physicists. They are happy to accept quantum mechanics as it presents itself in experiments and practical worldly applications—in other words, For All Practical Purposes (FAPP). But they are content to let the strangenesses implied by quantum theory (and its most accepted interpretations) molder away, bonelike, in the closet. They have fallen into what physicist John Bell called the FAPP trap.

As researchers Deepak Chopra, Menas Kafatos and Rudolph Tanzi have commented, "Most scientists, although respecting quantum theory, do not follow its implications. The result is a kind of schizophrenia between what scientists believe and what they practice."[30] And what they call schizophrenia, I simply call Blindspot.[*]

Yet even so, a definite rattling can be heard today in certain scientific circles. And it comes from a number of closeted skeletons whose existence cannot be denied forever. For there are six primary areas in which quantum theory corresponds perfectly with the revelations that become available from the nondual perspective. Admittedly, to list them here is a reckless proposition, as each one could take a textbook to support, but I'm going to make an attempt anyway. If I be guilty of simplification, at least I'm doing it intentionally. Simplicity, after all, is one of the prime signatures of nonduality. For reality itself is precisely *that which couldn't be simpler.*

As I proceed with my list of six, however, it might be useful to keep in mind that what I mean by "consciousness" might be equivalent to what a physicist might call "nothing," given the understanding that that very nothing has some explosively pregnant potentials for creative display.[†] And when I hear physicists employ terms such as "virtual particles," "quantum foam," and "Higgs field," I can't dismiss the possibility that they might also be referring to something close to what I am calling consciousness. I just don't possess the expertise to make the case either way. My interest in consciousness lies in its relevance to life and living in and as That—as experienced in human beings as happiness, peace, and beauty. Whereas for the scientific researcher, her

---

* And any blind spot in science trickles down into the general worldview of the age.

† See Laurence Krauss: *A Universe from Nothing: Why There Is Something Rather Than Nothing.*

favored terms reflect her interest in how these are relevant to her work. A work that, although often ecstatic, is not necessarily animated in her everyday life.

Let's take care of Blindspot Number 1, first: *Reductionism.*

If you dig deeply enough into any natural phenomenon, be it physical, chemical, biological, or cosmological, you hit quantum mechanics. This must be so, because quantum mechanics deals with the behavior of subatomic thingamajigs (particles, waves or "wavefunctions"), and *everything*—every "thing"—is ultimately "made" of these subatomic thingamajigs. But as is (almost) common knowledge by now, these elementary doohickeys are hard to pin down. They present some behaviors that are impossible to account for, rationally.

Even so far, this should sound familiar: If you dig deeply enough into exoteric religious belief systems, you will eventually hit nondual truth. And whether you're digging into exoteric religion or material physicality, what you find there in either case won't fit easily into rational boxes. As seminal physicist Niels Bohr said of his discoveries: "Unless you're shocked by quantum mechanics, you have not understood it."

Forgive my presumptuousness, but I think he probably meant to say that you will *never* understand it, no matter how shocked you may be. But if you get the *implications* of it, that will be enough to daze you. To wit: Quantum mechanics explodes the materialistic/reductionist view that all complex systems can be broken down into their ultimate simple parts. A conclusion that happens to be completely congruent with the nondual perspective.

The nondual is called such because from its perspective (as well as "in" its perspective and "as" its perspective), there is only one seamless happenstance ever going on. In its most absolute condition—its state of repose, you might say—this All One (no)Thing has no qualities, whatsoever. It is, literally, Nothing. And nothing whatsoever can be said about this Absolute, although both nondual teachings and quantum theory do point to it.[*] Hard to believe, but via some fancy quantum-theoretical tap dancing, it can even be argued that the entire universe sprang from, literally, this very same Nothing, entirely eliminating the need for turtles (which is a relief).[†]

Yet however it happens, as soon as anything arises into phenomenal manifestation from out of this reposed Absolute, it can be said to possess certain qualities. And the most fundamental of those qualities is awareness. As you know, nondual realizers often call this aware (no) Thing, "consciousness." This is also the word most commonly used in nondual circles in place of "God," because it best encapsulates that most evocative of its qualities—lucid awareness, pure intelligence, or pure subjectivity (without need for any objects).

So, given all this, here's the usual reductionistic question: Where can you find consciousness in a brain neuron? How does mind or consciousness emerge from mere matter?[‡] Such is the venerable conundrum of both philosophy and neurobiology, its "hard problem," which has occupied the prefrontal cortices of many a brilliant thinker over the past few hundred years. But from the nondual perspective the entire question is viewed as miscast: Consciousness is *not* an epiphenomenon of the brain, and therefore cannot be found by looking

---

* The term "Godhead" is used in some spiritual teachings to refer to the Absolute, as distinct from God. And the Absolute, or Godhead, about which nothing can be said, is actually neither nondual nor dual, neither existing nor non-existing, etcetera.

† Just how much nothing such a nothingness may be, however, is a matter of some dispute among physicists. But then, there's nothing about which physicists will not argue amongst themselves.

‡ When scientists use the word "mind," they use it interchangeably with "consciousness"; whereas in nondual circles, "mind" usually refers to the faculties of the separative ego and "consciousness" refers to That which illumines those faculties, existing prior to them.

deeper and deeper *in* the brain. First of all, because it is not exclusively personal, no matter whether in a human being or a bat.*

When neurobiologists attempt to tease out the existence of consciousness from the intimacies of the neuron, they define their target as "conscious experience." Using the latest marvels of brain scanning technology, they attempt to track the "neural correlates" in wet meat with the person's subjective sense of having an experience. But such an undertaking is fraught with Blindspotted error. An experience may be occurring for the laboratory subject, yet the consciousness out of which it arises is not traceable by this means. Consciousness is capable of being aware of one thing only—itself.† And whatever this means, it is *not* any kind of experience, to begin with. Consciousness is a complete collapse of experienc*er*-with-experienc*ing*-with-what is being experienc*ed*. It is the union of that which knows with the means of its knowing with the objects that are known. It is the union of perceiver-perception-perceived—the union of three elements that were never three to begin with.‡ And whatever may be traceable about it on a scan, it's not the part of experience that reveals consciousness, nor is whatever may be personal about it solely personal.

Check it out. You can approach another person, say, and attempt to find out the nature of his lived experience. You observe him in minute detail, as you creep closer and closer to him. Your observations get even more detailed and elaborated, the closer you creep, but you still haven't nailed down the exact nature of his subjective experience. So now

---

* Apologies to philosopher Thomas Nagel, who had a thing about bats (even if they weren't necessarily vampires).

† Consciousness is always conscious of itself, but in a human being it's modulated in the appearances of thinking, feeling, sensing and perceiving—while remaining nothing but itself all along.

‡ Nearing death, the sage J. Krishnamurti reminded his students, "You are the teacher, the taught and the teaching. You are the book of life." And this might also be one way that the Christian Trinity might be interpreted, esoterically.

you enlist the aid of technological "eyes" and "ears" for yourself and, keeping your subject still "ahead" of you, you creep closer and closer, down to the most precise, subatomic level, even. You have succeeded in identifying and measuring the finest details of your subject's synaptic firings. You have collected reams of printouts covered with meaningful figures. You have subjected these figures to the analyses of the best of today's AI bots. Yet have you really reached the heart of the matter? Have you really been able to bridge the gap between those printed figures and someone's actual conscious experience, as it is *lived*? Have you solved the old hard problem of bodymind philosophy?

From the nondual perspective, you cannot really solve the problem until you turn around 180 degrees and actually stand in your subject's shoes, as it were. Until suddenly your subject, who had been acting as your laboratory object, becomes your true, shared subject. You can creep up as close as your technology allows, but until you turn around and back up into *him*, dissolving all distance, you will not solve the problem of consciousness. And then, what you find will not be a "thing" at all. But whatever it is, it is exactly the same for that other person as it is for you.

What had been your laboratory object has now become your shared, impersonal subject. Pure Subjectivity, the one and only. The quantum question of where the dividing line is between the observer and that which is observed, is collapsed, because now it is seen that on the level of consciousness, there *is* no dividing line.*

So, when researchers attempt to find the neural correlates of consciousness in anyone's brain, they might be on the trail of something, for sure, but whatever it is, it ain't consciousness itself. Conscious awareness, from the nondual perspective, pervades *all* of existence, and is prior to the arising of any so-called personal experience—even

* Fascinating, that we should call the human objects of our clinical studies, "subjects." The underground esoteric influence hidden in the Blindspot can leak out in surprising ways.

though personal experience is illuminated by that same conscious awareness.

And that impersonal, all-pervading consciousness does not arise as a certain specific mixture of matter—a certain special brew of chemistry and biology. It's the other way around: It's consciousness that gives rise to matter, to brain and nematode. Consciousness—a name for intelligent awareness, if you will—is *prior* to any arisings in the form of any phenomenon. Which might be similar to the "aboutness" that those information theorists are searching for.

If this sounds like I've just made an argument for the old exoteric God in fancy terms, well, I must admit to a little fib here. From the nondual perspective, consciousness is not actually prior to phenomenal manifestation, as if it were standing apart from it. That's just a convenient way of expressing it, making it more understandable to the linear mind. But the reality is that it's all happening at once. And that once is...*Now*. Which means out of space/time, altogether. Only from the perspective of a (fictitious) self can there arise time and space, to begin with. Indeed, the very experience of a self is only definable by the edifices of time and space that constellate around it in a mutually adapted way. Prior to that apparently personal arising (just as prior to the Big Bang itself), time and space are...*not*.

The religiously educated might call that imponderable not-ness, when applied to time, Eternity, and that term would be as good as any, as long as you don't mistake it as meaning endless duration. When applied to space, you could call it Infinity, as long as you don't mistake it as meaning boundless dimension. The Absolute in repose (Nothing) and the Absolute in action (Everything) are two sides of the exact same coin, inseparable from each other and occurring all *at once* and all *at here*...in a mutually adapted way. The notion of some supernatural prior Entity with causal, omniscient powers simply does not fit in this picture.

No matter how you cut or scan the brain, however, consciousness cannot be an epiphenomenon of mushy tissue; it's the other way around. You can't get to consciousness by dissecting matter into finer and finer pieces of proto-neuron or microtubule. Just as you can't get to *you* by slicing up tinier and tinier pieces of chromosome. So there. Moreover, as the information theorists agree, you can't even get to *matter* by slicing up finer and finer pieces of matter. Whew. So much for scientific Blindspot #1: the principle of *Reductionism*.

Two steps forward, one step back. Even if we take the position that each person's experience of consciousness is uniquely her own...even then, the principle of reductionism breaks down. As physicist Theresa Bullard puts it, "All that can really be said thus far with the various brain imaging and mapping research is that certain brain regions *interact* with and *correspond* to certain functions of consciousness."[33] But this is far different from saying that consciousness somehow *emerged* from brain tissue and wouldn't exist without the latter's being there first. Which is nothing short of back-assward.

I'm harping on the reductionism thing because it represents such a fundamental assumption that most of us carry about reality. And like most notions we've inherited from classical physics, it seems to make sense: all big things can be broken down into the littler things of which they are composed. But when it comes to something as little (read: *subtle*) as consciousness—or quantum foam—this model doesn't hold up; and everything that makes sense proves to be nothing but shielding for the Blindspot. "Asking the brain to understand where [consciousness] comes from," says Deepak Chopra, "is like asking a robot to dismantle itself to find out what it's made of—you won't have a machine after the dismantling is done and, therefore, no answer."[34]

To solve the hard problem of consciousness by searching for the neurological correlates of experience in the brain—which is the scientific way of going about asking the question *Who am I?*—is tantamount to dismantling the robot. You may come up with many pretty colors on your MRI scans that way, but you'll never find out how those colors translate into someone's delight with the smells of her garden, someone's repulsion for the taste of anchovies, someone's getting a joke, or not...someone's unique sense of themselves *as* a self, existing in the world. As usual, Chopra gets the last word: "If you measured the body heat of Romeo and Juliet, that would be productive...yet the actual reality of romantic love doesn't appear as data."[35]

To respond to this challenge, Chopra and his colleagues propose a new field of study—"qualia science"—to investigate the confluences between what seem like moments of personal experience (*qualia*) and universal consciousness. To the extent that such an effort may also shed light on the Blindspot, it's a step in the right direction. For now, it's enough to make just one conclusive statement: Regardless of whether you take consciousness to be impersonal (which it is from the strictly nondual perspective) or personal (which it is from a person's subjective perspective)...it ain't gonna be found in matter, as long as that matter is taken to be an object with a separate and autonomous existence of its own. Again: so much for the principle of *Reductionism*.

Probably the most hair-pulling of all quantum mechanical puzzles is illustrated by the classic "two-slit" experiment or its "box-pair" variant. Neither of which am I going to describe here—save for the fact that they have probably pushed more skeletons into more closets than any other experiments in all of science. For good reasons: They seem to deny the existence of an objective reality that is out-there, separate from in-here—i.e., whoever is observing it. This proposition should sound familiar to you, my dear now-initiated quantum/nondualist reader. For not only does the two-slit experiment seem to obliterate the previously assumed borderline between an objective reality and a subjective observer, but it also argues that the observer *in here* may actually *determine* what happens in the so-called objective reality *out there*. And determines it by making choices...beforehand or afterhand, doesn't matter.

Simply put, these experimental results suggest that by observing something someplace, you create its being there. Which conclusion is congruent with the nondual perspective that any objective reality is knowable only within the limits of whatever perceptual faculties are employed to observe it. A human being will observe it one way, a bat another way, a Martian still another way. It is created in the image of its perceiver. But that "it"—objective reality itself—will remain unknown and unknowable as an object.

So, knock off Blindspot Number 2: *The Reality of Physical Reality*. Are you, like Niels Bohr, "shocked" yet?

Ah, but we've only just begun. Blindspot #3, #4, and #5—*Linear Causation, Free Will/Determinism,* and *Counterfactual Definiteness*—are intertwined so intimately that we will consider them in a package, as follows...

The infamous two-slit experiment (not to mention Schrödinger's scandalous cat*) also leads to the inescapable conclusion that there can be no such thing as free will. Yet at the same time, there can also be no such thing as determinism. Without going into a lot of digressive detail, let's just say that the observer of these experiments does get to choose how the experiment is set up, and it does seem like it's a free choice, at that. But once the experiment has passed a certain point of no return and one set of results have been produced—and *only* at that point—it becomes clear that this was the only possible choice that could ever have *been* made. Any protest that the observer could have freely chosen differently is simply not supportable by any

* Another famous quantum experiment (in thought only) whose description here would be a digression that would contribute little to my devious ends.

theoretical construct. Now, is that an argument *for* free will or *against* it? (Blindspot #4: *Free Will/Determinism*)

But wait. *Stop*. It's so easy to miss the nondual boat. This business about just what we mean by "the observer" keeps popping up, both in quantum mechanics and along the esoteric path. Physicists have taken great pains to refine the definition of observer and, as usual, have fallen into several competing camps in the process. Indeed, those who subscribe to the Many-Worlds interpretation of quantum theory resolve the entire puzzle of the "observer who's doing the measuring" in ways that boggle the mind even more than the standard (Copenhagen) interpretation. Yet even without going down that rabbit hole, we might ask: just how far back or how macroscopic or how removed from the quantum experiment does any observer need to be in order to truly merit the name? These may seem like fair questions. Nevertheless, on the ultimate level (which, remember, is Truth, which is Reality), *there is no separate entity to begin with. The whole imagined notion of an observer as a freely deciding entity is just an academic exercise for the debating team; as far as actual reality goes, it bears little relationship.*

From the nondual perspective (which is also in alignment with quantum theory, once released from the closet), the so-called observer and that which is observed are embraced in a dance of inconceivable interrelatedness. If a tree falls in the forest, something may have occurred, whether you heard it or not. But...

Whatever that something is, outside of our respective (probably very different) experiences of it (*qualia*), it is completely unknowable. If nobody was around to hear the falling tree, the question of whether or not the tree actually fell becomes not only not answerable, but not deserving an answer. The entire question of the actuality of the falling tree, divorced from any hearer, becomes moot—and sophomoric, besides. (Blindspot #6: *Separability*, amplified next chapter)

Moreover, while the falling of some trees may be more or less probable than the falling of other trees, none of the falling is being "caused" in any sense in which we use that word.

According to the late physicist John Wheeler, "All things physical are information-theoretic in origin."[36] Anticipating the pronouncements of the information theorists, he meant that hidden, abstract information is more fundamental than any physical thing. In nondual terms, all this means is that the cause of any *one* thing happening in the universe is...*everything else*. Every arising phenomenon is both the cause and the effect of its own arising, as is every other phenomenon in the cosmic system—in an interwoven, endlessly entangled, implicate, co-emergent, winking-in, winking-out, holographic complexity of infinite echoes, on and on without end, Amen. And it's all happening at once, from, in, and as consciousness.* (Blindspot #3: *Linear Causation.*)

From that perspective, there can be no such thing as free will, because there is no separate, independent observer, to begin with. The question itself, "Do I have free will," is misconceived, because, once again, it blind-spottedly assumes the existence of a *me* who could ever possess such a thing or not.

Yet as well: When that which we call the observer seems to determine the result of the two-slit experiment by making what appears to be a free choice about the experimental design, this also has a certain truth to it. It may be one step down, as it were, from the ultimate view of things, but that's okay, for otherwise we'd have nothing whatsoever to say about it. And that would be no fun.

And since we all enjoy talking, we can answer that vexing question, "Do you have free will?" with a Yes—but only as long as you insist on the personal volition of an individual entity called *me*. Do you *not* have free will? Yes. But only when you awaken to the fact that that *you* (along with its volition) is a fiction.

Even so, nonduality is only truly nondual when it is not merely relegated to some transcendental escapist realm, washing its hands of

---

* And the driving force behind this holy mess is Love. But that's another story, a different book.

the so-called relative world; but when it recognizes both the worldly and the transcendent as not different from each other. The sage who remains in the worldly cave of amusements (and terrors) is able to play in either perspective without getting lost in conditioned interpretations. The Yaqui sorcerer Don Juan called such play "controlled folly." *Whatever we call* true *is only true in reference to the domain of reality in which you are playing at any given time—as long as you can* see *it that way.*

An analogy often made in esoteric teachings is that of the coiled rope versus a snake. From a distance, or at dusk, you may easily mistake the former for the latter, and you will immediately be seized by fear. However, if you can summon the nerve to approach the apparent snake, you will soon recognize that it wasn't actually a snake at all, but rather just a coiled rope. At that point you may still see the *appearance* of a snake, but it will no longer fool you. You can relax, for now you know that it is a really a rope.

The appearance of the snake belongs to the domain of the relative; the actuality of it belongs to the domain of reality. Once you have awakened to reality, you may still experience—and enjoy—the appearances that populate the relative, but you are no longer in thrall to them. You can play at controlled folly. "Maya still dances, but it is a dance of love not seduction."* [37]

Hence, the nondual response to Blindspot #4—*Free Will vs. Determinism*—is Yes: both are true, but only from their respective points of perspective.

Just to make things a bit more interesting, however, the implications of either view about free will also denies something called "counterfactual definiteness" in both philosophy and physics. Whether we take the deterministic position or the nondeterministic position with regard to our choices, all the experimental evidence supports the conclusion that whatever we (the observer) decide, we could not have

---

* Maya being the personified image of illusion in both Hinduism and Buddhism.

decided differently. As previously noted, the sense that the researcher who sets up the parameters of the two-slit experiment *could* have chosen one way or another just ain't so. The sense that we *could* have chosen chocolate rather than vanilla—when in fact we chose vanilla—is false. In reality, we could *not* have chosen anything other than what we *did* choose. The sense that we could have chosen differently is mistaken—*although this becomes the case only after the fact.*[*] (Blindspot #5: *Denial of Counterfactual Definiteness.*)

In esoteric spiritual teachings this same principle is often articulated to sum up the entire nondual enterprise in one succinct declaration: "What is, *is*, as it is."

And there it is, in a nutshell—the entire world library of nondual transmissions. If the seeker were to really *get* this one deceptively simple axiom, and to cease arguing with it, she would simultaneously get the whole enchilada. Even to merely believe this fundamental fact about the truth of things can bestow upon any seeker a great sense of relief.

What is, is, *as it is.*

And so it is that in one fell swoop we have wrapped up...

Blindspot Number 3, *Linear Causation*

Blindspot Number 4, *Free Will/Determinism*

and Blindspot Number 5, *Counterfactual Definiteness*

Added to...

Blindspot Number 1, *Reductionism*

and Blindspot Number 2, *Reality of Physical Reality*

I'll leave you with the words of Isaac Bashevis Singer: "You have to believe in free will. You have no choice."

---

[*] See the two-slit experiment and think Schrödinger's Cat, while rubbing your tummy and chewing your gum.

XIII

SIX BLIND SPOTS, PART 2

So far, we've established that the cause of any one thing happening in the universe is everything else. To quote physicist Anton Zeilinger:

> We have tried for centuries to look deeper and deeper into finding causes and explanations, and suddenly, when we go to the very depths, to the behavior of individual particles or individual quanta, we find that this search for a cause comes to an end. There is no cause. In my eyes, this fundamental indeterminateness of the universe has not really been integrated into our worldview yet.[38]

Although the mind wants to ascribe some kind of First Cause or "the cause of all causes"—usually imagined as God—to anything that came into existence without any apparent precedent, the quantum physical view does not support this unprovable and non-rigorous assumption. And neither does the nondual perspective.

From the quantum physical view, stuff just happens—albeit as the result of some highly complicated theoretical razzmatazz. Sometimes the stuff that happens seems probable and sometimes the stuff that happens seems improbable. But none of it is caused by some kind of prior creator (which itself had no prior cause, unless it was an especially magic turtle). The human, mind-mediated sense of causation emerges like a dream from the realm of the non-causal. That this view has "not really been integrated" into our cultural consensus may be just Zeilinger's polite way of saying Blindspot.

In any case, to say that there is no cause (quantum mechanics) is actually the same as to say that the cause of any one thing happening in the universe is everything else (nonduality). Because if the cause of any one thing happening in the universe is everything else, then eventually every effect in this vast entangled web of Everything must eventually become the cause of something else, which in turn must itself become another effect of another cause, and on and on, *ad infinitum*, with no beginning and no end, backwards and forwards, too.* Might as well just say, "No cause."

But then this also means that every arisen manifestation in the system is just as responsible for the entire creation as every other arisen manifestation in the system. It's impossible to tease out of this infinite tangle any one causal entity to point a finger at. And now, finally, perhaps you might see that even to ask that hoary question of theodicy doesn't make any sense. At this level, the issue is essentially meaningless. Who or what could you possibly blame for any occurrence?

I cautioned you in the first chapter how circular the entire consideration of this book might appear. Well, I think I have fulfilled that promise. But as uncomfortable as this view might make you or me, we can't argue with reality. Or, if we do, we will lose the argument…every time.

I also promised that the nondual answer to the question of theodicy would be surpassingly simple, and I've kept my word by delivering something even simpler: *pointlessness.*

I have already used the word "entangled" without defining it, although it has become widely used in pop-scientific expression. Speaking pop-scientifically, it means that any object that has ever interacted with

---

* Described as "interdependent co-arising" in Buddhism and metaphorically by the Hindu/Buddhist image of Indra's Net.

another object—which includes *every* object, because everything was in intimate contact with everything else during the first moments of the universe—is foreverafter enmeshed with the other, at least on the subatomic level: What happens to one quantum doohickey (as soon as it's measured), happens also to the other—either instantaneously or not, depending on which physicist you ask.. This has been demonstrated experimentally over and over. We may know that the sum of the spins of a pair of related particles is zero, for example, but neither of them possesses a definite spin direction until one of them is measured, "causing" the other particle to assume the opposite spin direction. More or less instantly. Even though the particles may be physically separated by light years. And even though no physical force connects the two. Such is the mysterious feature that has been dubbed "entanglement."

In the 1980s, physicist John Bell's experiments confirmed the entanglement predictions of quantum theory—that so-called objects could not have properties that are separately their own, independent from each other. Here is how physicists Fred Kuttner and Bruce Rosenblum describe the implications of this finding:

> In principle...any two objects that have ever interacted are forever entangled. The behavior of one instantaneously influences the other, and the behavior of everything entangled with it. Since macroscopic objects are almost impossible to isolate, they rapidly become entangled with everything else in their environment. The effect of such complex entanglement generally becomes undetectable. Nevertheless, there is, in principle, a universal connectedness whose meaning we have yet to understand. We can indeed "see the world in a grain of sand."[39]

Einstein may have had difficulty accepting these "spooky actions" (as he called them), but by now you should not. It's simple nondual truth, is it not?

Sure, in quantum mechanical interpretations beyond the standard one, the picture of entanglement becomes more complicated, involving a sister mechanism called decoherence. Yet even if you buy those models, the notion that anything can be independently removed from anything else still breaks down. And although some physicists argue that the speed demanded by entangled communication cannot be faster than that of light, nondual spirituality explodes the entire edifices of "speed" and "distance" to begin with. You might think, therefore, that science and spirituality deviate from each other in this regard. But then again, it is well to remember that quantum mechanical science is still in its adolescence, and much remains to be discovered.

And so much for Blindspot Number 6: *Separability*. That is: Within the One (no)Thing, how can anything be separate from anything else? And consequently, how can anything that seems to happen at a distance not really be happening in a spaceless Here? And how can anything that seemed to be happening "then" not really be happening in a timeless Now?

And if you think about it (a dangerous proposition), with the collapse of Separability, Blindspots #1 through #5 must also be simultaneously collapsed. No Separability, then no Reductionism, no Physical Reality, no Linear Causation, no Determinism, no Counterfactual Definiteness. Yes, entangled we all live, entangled we all die—even though what we call living cannot be something opposed to dying. John Bell himself recognized how unreasonable his own experimental conclusions were. "The quantum mechanical description will be superseded," he predicted, by some new, hitherto undreamed-of way of understanding reality. And "this way of seeing things will involve an imaginative leap that will astonish us."[40]

I can't help quoting Jesus here:

> The seeker should not stop until he finds. When he does find, he will be disturbed. After having been disturbed, he will be *astonished*. Then he will reign over everything." (Gospel of Thomas; italics mine)

I'm sure that some of you, dear readers, may have already voiced the objection (loudly, to your dog) that much of what I'm saying could be extrapolated to support the discredited philosophical principle of solipsism—the idea that there is no reality other than the reality that you—and I'm talkin' to *you*—experience, yourself. The absurdity of this proposition has often been called "silly solipsism" in academia.

As Australian comic Tim Minchin put it: "My last words are going to be, 'Who's the world going to revolve around now?'"

Yes, solipsism may indeed be silly, but from the nondual perspective, it happens to be true—well, sort of. More precisely stated: If there is some reality outside of your own experience of reality, you can *never* know it, or even suspect *that* it exists. If a tree falls in the forest, but you're not there to hear it, it's completely nonsensical to ask whether or not it makes a sound: The very falling of it is inaccurately stated, to begin with:

What sound? *What* tree?

The so-called tree cannot make a sound, because for that to happen a perceiver must experience an associated vibration striking his eardrum. And if there's no sound, the question of a tree becomes moot. Which does not mean that neither sound nor tree exists, but just that that's something that can't be known. Even your husband, even your daughter, your mother (your hands, your genitals...) may all just be figments of your imagination, you'll never know for sure. Just as in quantum theory, each tiny chunk of energy is called a *quantum*, so can we call each tiny chunk of subjective experience a *qualia*—which is where Deepak Chopra's qualia science comes in.

From the qualia-scientific perspective, rocks—as objective things themselves—are not hard, nor is water wet or sugar sweet. They are nothing but qualia created in consciousness, using a particular observer's brain as a processing medium. The seemingly obvious assumption that an objective reality exists (somewhere out there) turns out to be just not so. Nothing exists except the energy of awareness, modulating itself into an appearance that can be experienced by an attuned medium (perhaps *you*). Just as quantum theory has proven that no object, whatever its size, has any fixed properties outside the context of its observation, so does qualia science attempt to define what, exactly, that observational context *is*.

I wish those qualia scientists luck. From here, it seems more than enough to realize that 1) reality is entirely contextual in nature, 2) that qualia are the building blocks of that context, and 3) that qualia themselves are rooted in (and made *of*) consciousness. These not-really-solipsistic principles are wonderful expressions of humanity's latest attempts to finally unlock that fusty old mind-body (or spirit-matter) problem.

From the nondual perspective, it's just not necessary to take the question any further. It's quite possible, I suppose, that scientists may succeed in defining in ever-more precise detail the quantum mathematical interface between neurological firings and subjective experience. But it always boils down to the one same thing: qualia (the experiences experienced by the scientists-acting-as-subjects) experiencing qualia (the experiences experienced by the scientists-acting-as-objects). While all the while, the consciousness in which all such qualia arise, stay awhile, and disappear can never be understood by any qualia that are probing it. Which is just fine, for the condition of nondual enlightenment is precisely the condition of not-knowing.

If your eyes are glazing over at this point, you can relax. Once again, as always, the only final question is *Who is experiencing what?* The solipsism of philosophy is silly only insofar as it still assumes an experiencer who is a separate entity with its own independent subjectivity; it always comes down to that illusion, in the Blindspot. But by now we should know better. And I'll let the teacher Rupert Spira sum it up:

> Experience is not experienced by something outside of, separate from, or other than itself. Nor does experience

> ever come in contact with anything other than itself, such as a separate, independently existing object, self or world. Experience just experiences itself—one unnamable, indivisible whole, simultaneously knowing and being itself alone.[41]

Even if it might not be the most ultimate view of things, however, the sense most of us have that we can and do experience our own experiences, make our own decisions, and have to deal with the consequences of them, is entirely appropriate *at that level* of awakening consciousness. Once again, the denial of free will or counterfactual definiteness is *descriptive* of ultimate reality, not *prescriptive*. It does not imply that anyone should suddenly absolve herself of any responsibility for her actions, or that we should defund our criminal justice system. The truth that the so-called individual *me* is not actually the doer of her actions, is not meant as an instruction to just sit on the couch all day, paralyzed by some nondual concepts about the fundamental illusion of any personal experience or choice.*

Similarly, the sense we might have that an oncoming bus could run us over, is also entirely appropriate. The description of an ultimate truth in which physical reality is not real should not be taken as encouragement for us to dash out heedless into traffic.

At the same time, however, if we could sense even the flavor of these reality-challenging ideas, it might help us release our grip just a little bit more on the tiller of our lifeboat; that we may lift the blame from some imagined God—as well as anyone else—for all the bad things that happen to us or others; that we may let go of any regrets that may plague us over our supposed past mistakes; that we may even

---

* Jed McKenna's bumper sticker: *Pro-Choicelessness.*

recognize that calling them "mistakes" is not accurate. And to help us live this dream of existence with a more accepting attitude, here in our phantasmagorical dance with emptiness.

"Whatever it is that's arising in your experience," says teacher Christopher Wallis,

> ...in truth it's not a reward or a punishment...it's not deserved or undeserved, it wasn't ordained by some other being, it wasn't chosen by some earlier self of yours so that this self could learn a lesson, and it's not happening to fulfill a part in the story your mind wants to tell about your life: it's simply, beautifully, spontaneously, perfectly and completely expressing what you are. It has no other reason for being and needs no other reason.[43]

The assertions about reality that have arisen from quantum mechanics have been slow to trickle down into the general planetary worldview, even after a hundred years of discoveries. Most obviously, this may be because they defy commonsense appearance in so many ways, not to mention the convincing display of classical physics that we see operating all around us. But beyond that, they also seem to imperil all our standard egoic identifications with the separate, conditioned self—the "little me" who stands "in-here" as opposed to some vast imagined reality "out-there." In short, the general culture resists embracing quantum physics for the same reasons why most people keep esoteric spirituality in the Blindspot. It's not that it's so unreasonable or un-understandable. It's that it's just too damn threatening. It's that third rail of culture again, the "taboo against knowing who you are."

Following his own actual encounter with his true, empty nature, research scientist Sperry Andrews became very curious. Was this some kind of general agreement that everybody around him had always held, but didn't ever talk about? Was it something that people just took for granted, but he had just discovered? "Could there be some socially acceptable, commonly sensed intelligence about 'this'?" Quizzing the folks around him, he got his answer soon enough:

> Would my closest friends or family understand? No! No one seemed to know what I was talking about. There seemed to be a lack of interest to explore or even try to comprehend who or what we are. I have to say, it was perplexing.[42]

Andrews is certainly not the only one to have run up against this general indifference. The famous case of Suzanne Segal is representative of this scenario.* Following her spontaneous "loss of self" in 1982, she spent the next 14 years running from psychologist to psychiatrist, collecting pathological diagnoses and sinking into deeper and deeper despair...until finally meeting some folks (Buddhists, as it happens) who instantly recognized what was going on with her. Although today it might not have taken her quite as long to find someone who could properly diagnose her condition, her case remains paradigmatic of the general Blindspot of which I speak.

It's only from the viewpoint afforded by an awakening to true nature that this widespread avoidance of the void can be clearly seen: how so many billions of beings are racing away, faster and faster, from That which can never be escaped. Yet it's the very act of racing, itself—the fixation of attention and energy on "I-me-mine" in an ever-speeding whirlpool of self-obsessed acquisitiveness and multiplication—which is at the root of all the planetary problems that we say we want to solve, all the human and nonhuman misery that we say we want to heal. And

---

* Referencing her 1996 book, *Collision with the Infinite: A Life Beyond the Personal Self.*

it all comes back down to our futile racing away from that which is unavoidable: who we *are*. Sperry Andrews asks:

> Are we so identified with form and appearances, afraid of the radical nature of our freedom, of being "nobodies" going nowhere forever, that we have narrowed our choices? ...The single greatest oversight today might be missing the pivotal importance of a self/Self-referencing Void.[44]

What he calls oversight I call Blindspot. And save for those few bridging insights nibbling around its edges, the Blindspot remains rife in our global society today, showing up in everything from an economics that cannot find its way off the hamster wheel of unsustainable growth to a politics vacillating between authoritarian suppression and hyperpartisan paralysis...from a pop culture that raises the drama of personal dilemma to the level of hysterical apotheosis to a model of human psychology that reduces it to insurance-billable numbers. And always, what we see, what we cleave to, how we model our perceptions...is exactly what we get, 'round and around on that ol' grinding wheel of *samsara*.

Which leads me, somehow, to NOMA.

I hate to break this to you, but there's no such thing as Non-Overlapping Magisteria. Yes, with my usual humility, I will even quibble with the eminent Stephen Jay Gould (who's not around anymore to argue back).

The late evolutionary biologist made the case that religion and science were not inherently incompatible with each other. The apparent conflict between these two magisteria, as he called them, was foolish and unnecessary, because...

> the magisterium of science covers the empirical realm: what is the universe made of (fact) and why does it work that way (theory)? The magisterium of religion extends over questions of ultimate meaning and moral value. These two magisteria do not overlap...[45]

Gould called this equal-but-separate viewpoint Non-Overlapping Magisteria, or NOMA, and said that the magisteria of religion and science held "equal worth and necessary status for any complete human life; [yet]...remain logically distinct and fully separate lines of inquiry."

Thus can science and religion live side-by-side in complete autonomy and self-respect; any apparent need to make a choice between them is gratuitous. This perspective has been widely adopted by most thinking people today as a nice, neat way of addressing an often-divisive issue, applying the highest values of liberal humanism to it. Prestigious Templeton prizes have been won by advocates of NOMA.

And it sounds reasonable enough, too. But is it true?

Well, maybe—but only if by "religion" we're talking about the usual exoteric kind, based upon beliefs and handed-down prescriptions. If the magisterium of religion is one in which beliefs are held (fervently) and questions of morality are debated (exoterically), then yes, it does make sense to see it as a certain bounded domain of human endeavor, quite distinct from the domain of science. But if this is the case, then the whole conflict between science and religion has nothing to do with truth or God, anyway, so is not worth arguing about, whether or not their respective magisteria are overlapping.

If we define religion as esoteric spirituality, however, then we have something worth our consideration. Even though we must then conclude that there is no such thing as non-overlapping magisteria—or non-overlapping anything else, for that matter. Religion, in this sense, is not some alternative way of knowing among several other possible ways. It is *the* way...

...of *not* knowing. It is Not-Knowing itself.

Here we go again:

Truth is not magisterial at all. It is That in which *all* magisteria arise—science, religion, sports, music, pornography...you name it (Blindspot #6: *Separability*). Put in Zen Buddhist terms, it is the "suchness"—the nonperceptible intimacy—of all possible magisteria. It is the suchness of the brain's synaptic firings, and the suchness of the fMRI that is recording them, and the suchness of the researcher who is interpreting the data. It is the suchness of every neural correlate of consciousness. It is Brahman (Hinduism); it is Planck-scale spacetime geometry (quantum physics); it is the texture of Plato's Forms; it is the implicate order (Bohm); it is the field of infinite potentiality (Chopra); it is Fathersonholyspirit.

It is the dreaming (Australian Aboriginal).

XIV

THE DARK SIDE

WARNING: Should the following data be not already known to you, brace yourself (once again) for astonishment.

The observable universe—this incomprehensibly vast throng of galaxies ("billions and billions" of them, as sorely missed Carl Sagan once said), each consisting of billions and billions of stars, all scattered in a space of incomprehensible dimensions...this utterly mind-boggling immensity of matter and energy...accounts for a mere *five percent* of the total universe.

Five percent. So say our astrophysicists. Everything we can see, measure, account for with our own senses or that of our finest technological instruments: a measly five percent (within a few percentage points).

Five percent!

So, what could the other 95 percent of the universe be possibly made of? Well...approximately 70 percent so-called "dark energy" and another 25 percent "dark matter."

What?

Dark energy and dark matter are not easy to describe, as the fact of their existence at all can only be inferred by what we *can* see or measure. But the physicists know that they must be present in order for their calculations about the age of the universe (when the Big Bang happened), plus the speed of universal expansion, plus the nature of the gravitational forces working on that expansion, plus some other fancy stuff...to come out right.

To rephrase: Dark energy and dark matter must be there—even though we don't know what the hell they are—in order for every other cosmological variable to make sense. They are the unobservable goblins needed for the mathematical equations about the observable universe to click (leaving aside the theoretical possibility of other, multiple universes). As described by physicist Laurence Krauss:

> We are now virtually certain that the dark matter—which...has been independently corroborated in a host of different astrophysical contexts...—must be made of something new, something that doesn't exist normally on Earth. This kind of stuff, which isn't star stuff, isn't Earth stuff either. But it *is* something![46]

With regard to dark energy, he goes on to acknowledge that its origin and nature "is without a doubt the biggest mystery in fundamental physics today." All of which would not come as any surprise to any nondual realizer, for it makes perfect sense from that perspective—at least as an instructive metaphor.

The five-percent proportion that's accountable to the observable universe is perfectly analogous to the perceptual confinement of ego. When the self's identification is limited to its usual conditioned boundaries, it's as if that self is carrying a tiny flashlight as it toddles through the vastness of the universe. All it can perceive is limited to the pathetic beam of the flashlight, while just outside the beam, waiting all the while, is the fantastic vastness of the universe. *That* 95 percent of the universe is completely invisible—dark—to the egoic self. Just like the physicists with their equations, the seeker can infer—from the numerous testimonies of the sages throughout history, if not from her own personal glimpses—that something *must* exist outside her little beam, even though she doesn't know what it could be.

And that's the whole point. The vastness awaiting the seeker outside his little flashlight beam—outside the cave of his opinions, beliefs, habits, memories, conclusions, positions, morals, postures, defenses, masks, roles, mediated images—lies the Unknown, The Dark, which the Sufis describe as "dazzling." This is precisely what keeps most of us stuck, for more than anything, we crave the known, the familiar, the comfortable. Even our suffering—or especially that—we cling to because it's familiar territory; and we will cling to it with a death-grip (literally), rather than leap into the dark unknown. Into the Cloud of Unknowing, the Court of the Black Madonna, the Domain of Possibility, the "death before you die"...

Restricting ourselves to our pathetic little flashlight beam, we assume that what we perceive is all there is, while just beyond its glow, awaiting us all the while, is the vastness of the unknown 95 percent. We feel its presence, and some of us can actually hear its invitation, its calling, its still small voice. And when we follow its whispering lure, we finally step outside the cave and into the dazzling light of the universal dark. Which, we then discover, was never separate from, or outside of, or beyond, our familiar little glow, after all; but was rather thoroughly interpenetrating it, and shining *as* it, all along.*

No wonder the Blindspot has so often prevailed. The Whole—the One (no)Thing—is not visible, not perceivable with our usual instruments of perception, so we could pretend that it's not there. Just as people could pretend that the observable universe was all there is, until the astrophysicists of the twentieth century informed us otherwise. But how much longer can we play this game of obliviousness? Of willful ignorance? How much longer will we satisfy ourselves with such a pathetic flashlight beam of blinded perception? How much longer will we cling to our dear old comforting, nostalgic, familiar suffering?

And on this particular planet: How much longer will our batteries hold out?

---

* Which I predict will also happen, when the physicists finally manage to isolate dark energy and dark matter. They will discover its essentially interpenetrating, non-separatable nature apart from visible energy and matter.

XV

ANTHROPICALLY DIVINE

Here are a few of the ingredients of our cosmic soup that had to be "just right" in order for the conditions for life as we know it to emerge:

- Within seconds after the Big Bang, the quarks (thingamabobs needed to form atomic nuclei) would have had to suddenly gather in groups of three—two "ups" and one "down" (don't ask) to form protons, and two "downs" and one "up" to form neutrons. Which happened.
- The charges of these quarks would have had to be exactly 2/3 for each "up" quark and -1/3 for each "down" quark. Which happened.
- The masses of the first elementary particles that formed once the quarks had arranged themselves would have had to fit certain precise ratios. Which happened.
- The strengths of all the forces of nature—gravity, electromagnetism, the weak and strong nuclear forces, as well as the mysterious dark energy that permeates space—would all have had to observe certain precise values in order for the universe to neither collapse upon itself nor explode into smithereens. Which happened.

In short, there are approximately 200 physical parameters that must be precisely what they are, in order for stars to ignite and planets to form and all the elements…to be created. And that's not even considering the raft of other finely-tuned preconditions that must fall into place for life to rear its unlikely head. Yet every one of those stipulations for the creation of a universe capable of supporting life anywhere *were* met, despite the very long odds. They happened to happen: coincidence?

And beyond all the *hows* lie all the imponderable *whys*. We still don't know why the measurement of the strength of electromagnetic interactions is constant at 1/137. Or why the mass of the proton happens to be 1,836.153 times that of the electron. Or why Newton's gravitational constant is equal to 6.67384×10^{-11}. Moving on, we also have little idea how the complicated, eukaryotic cells in the bodies of living organisms emerged. Let alone how consciousness assumed the forms of self-awareness, intelligence, and...(drum roll, please) symbolic thinking. For that matter, although theories abound, we're not even sure what caused the Big Bang, to begin with.

In what I would call an understatement, Stephen Hawking said that "If one considered the possible constants and laws that could have emerged, the odds against a universe like that having produced life like ours, are immense."[47]

It might look like all these considerations sets the stage for Intelligent Design, waiting in the wings to make its triumphant entrance as the great cosmic *deus ex machina*, settling all our questions, once for all. But by now you should know that I will most assuredly *not* be relying on any such thing.

Of all the theories advanced by physicists and cosmologists to account for all the improbabilities that occurred for this universe to be as it is, the one that comes the closest to the nondual perspective is also the one with the least explanatory power. In fact, it just seems to beg the question. It goes by the name of the Anthropic Principle, and here it is, in a nutshell: *If the laws and constants of the universe were anything but the way they are, we wouldn't be here to consider them.*

It may be even stranger to consider that all the evidence that scientists have collected to account for everything in the universe being what it is, is only available in this particular period of time. Everything from how the universe is expanding to the existence of galaxies beyond our own, depends upon quantum evidence that did not even exist billions of years ago and will cease to exist billions of years hence. This is predictable, given a host of factors inherent in how the universe has expanded since the Big Bang, and will continue to expand into the future.

So, if any physicists happened to be around to perform their research that far in the past or will be around to perform their work billions of years in the future, the evidence available to them will drive them to completely different conclusions about the nature of the universe than present-day physicists have available to them. Thus, even though from a human timescale the current period is a very long one, it happens to be a weirdly propitious one. As Laurence Krauss puts it: "We live at a very special time…the only time when we can observationally verify that we live at a very special time!"[48] Which although perhaps only half-serious, is another way of stating the anthropic principle. "It is not too surprising," states Krauss, "to find that we live in a universe in which we can live."[49]

As usual in physics, the anthropic principle has stirred up plenty of controversy—with emphasis on the "con." After all, it really doesn't say anything more than that things are the way they are because they couldn't be any other way and still support our being here to ask the question. Not too satisfying to the mind, true, but remember, in nonduality it's not the mind we need to satisfy. Plus, its very circularity might be a mark of its truthiness.

Here's one way of picturing it, however: The Absolute (every possibility in repose, in a state of infinite potential) somehow decides to unfurl from within itself the energy of conscious creativity—Shakti/Eros—which then manifests in uncountable forms, performing uncountable actions, expressing uncountable moods, from the most beatific to the most terrifying. And all this, just so It can observe Itself in as many ways as possible. Just so It can enjoy the cosmic amusement park with as many rides as possible. All completely self-referential, indeed, whether the rides are speeding forward or backward. Yet even as this creative unfurling stuff is happening sequentially, the Absolute remains completely undisturbed all the while, which is no-while at all. The unfurling of forms (in time), in other words, happens coincidentally with the re-furling of forms into their absolute stillness (out of time). In the end, there is no difference between them. In all creative arisings, silence inheres. In all silence, creative arisings inhere. In Tantric terms: Shiva (the principle of unmanifest vibratory potential) and Shakti (the principle of creative expression) remain in full copulatory embrace, for all eternity.*

Does any of this support the anthropic principle? Yes, I would say, although not as it's usually formulated.

Given the mathematical quirks (and quarks) that support our universe, it seems that the universe is not just improbably hospitable to us (the weak anthropic principle), but downright tailor-made for us (the strong anthropic principle). Which of course it would *have* to be, if *we* were the ones who made it come into being in this (anthropic) way.

Physicist Hendrik Casimir appears to be arguing just this point when he says:

> Sometimes it almost appears that the theories [of quantum physics] are not a description of a nearly inaccessible reality, *but that that so-called reality is a* result *of the theory*. [italics mine][50]

Although I can't claim to know where Casimir was coming from when he said this, it appears that he is creeping close to another one

---

* Such an image is NOT meant to suggest that the term "tantric" refers only to sexual stuff. This is a common misperception that I don't want to reinforce, as there is actually *no* realm of human experience that Tantrism fails to address.

of those boggling quantum conclusions that happen to correspond so nicely with nondual ones. If we mix Casimir's statement with the above-cited Shiva-Shakti story, we can then go one step further: *To discover and to create is all one inseparable process. To discover something, and measure it, is to actually bring that thing into manifestation.*

Just as from the nondual perspective, the observer plus that-which-is-observed plus the act-of-observ*ing* are all one seamless happenstance, so too are the trio of discovering-measuring-creating. Yet another physicist, Marcelo Gleiser, puts it this way:

> In quantum physics, the trio consisting of the observer, the measuring device, and what is being measured form a new entity, which is described by a single wavefunction. As Schrödinger explained, their individual wavefunctions are "entangled." In principle, the whole Universe should be part of the description, given that all sorts of remote effects act on all of us...[51]

So, which came first: Planck's Quantum Constant ("out there," waiting to be discovered), or Max Planck's "discovery" of it? Which came first: Einstein's Energy Constant ("out there," waiting to be discovered), or Albert Einstein's "discovery" of it? Did the mathematical constants that came to bear the names of their discoverers even possess any existence before the discoverers tripped over them? And after the riddles of dark matter and dark energy are finally solved—i.e., discovered/measured/created—what will be the next final mystery that we will need to concoct for ourselves to keep us (aka consciousness) amused?

Yet the principle I'm endorsing here isn't merely anthropic. For if a man or woman knew who he or she actually *was*, if they awakened to their true nature, then the principle would not be called anthropic, no matter whether weak or strong. It would be called Anthropically Divine.

Useful as it is under everyday circumstances to say that the world exists out there independent of us, that view can no longer be upheld. There is a strange sense in which this is a "participatory universe."[52]

So asserted eminent physicist John Wheeler. According to Gleiser... "He [Wheeler] claimed that the act of measurement was more than mere observing: it determined how history would unfold from that point on (and even backwards!); it changed the universe."[53]

In this way, the Anthropically Divine principle implies some kind of participatory function at work in the creation of the universe, a partnership, even a co-creation going on. It's not a co-creation in which some fictitious me-self is involved, but rather your true nature. Just as the personal me cannot dictate what will actually be manifested in its personal life, so it is that the me cannot dictate what will be manifested in its co-creation with the All.* In that seminal two-slit experiment, the result is *random*. The observer may get to choose the game (the experimental design), but not the outcome. Never merely a separate, desiring entity, the observer is instantaneously entangled with nothing less than *Everything Else*—the Totality. Which was always his true condition, anyway: not a separate, self-existent entity at all, but rather one with that very same Whole.

Of course, the intuition of anthropic divinity cannot be entirely new if it has the fragrance of truth in it. According to historian Chris Cochran, the pivotal 16th century planetary theorist Johannes Kepler regarded scientific knowledge as "not something to be discovered, but recovered by the soul, in the process of doing science." Kepler understood the intellect to be like a divine participation rather than a strictly individual cognition. This view of intellect was different from the way we understand it today. Rather, Kepler saw learning as "a process of actualizing new aspects of the intelligence of God in the personal soul.[54]

---

* Any such co-creation thus bears no resemblance to similar-sounding New Age concepts—that I get to attract to myself what manifests in reality, simply by the way I use my desire-driven mind.

Which is just a beautiful way of expressing the same perennial insight: that the human acts of discovering and creating and measuring and observing are all interrelated in some kind of inconceivable cosmic hoedown. Such a difficult thing to reduce to words, this vision of reality, but that has not stopped nondual teachers from trying. Here's Ramesh Balsekar's attempt (twentieth century, Indian):

> The universe is uncaused
> Like a net of jewels
> In which each—each jewel—
> Is only the reflection
> Of all the others
> In a fantastic interrelated harmony
> Without end.[55]

And the so-called individual is not exempted, but is just another jewel/reflection, uniquely expressed as his- or herself. Such is the nature of Indra's Net, which is holographically echoing each and every element of itself and celebrating the information of every part, in an infinite dance of co-emergent arisings, *ad infinitum.*

No, you don't always get what you want. But the anthropically divine principle argues that you always get what you were going to get, once it has been gotten. If that's any comfort.

Just a word in acknowledgement here. Some physicists reject the evidence for any fine-tuning of the preconditions for the arising of life in the universe, arguing that all those apparently improbable values can be explained. And others (especially supporters of string theory) make the argument that the possible existence of multiple other universes evens the odds considerably for the emergence of life, both here and in uncountably many other places—life based on physical laws and energetic principles that we can't even imagine.

But not only do neither of these propositions contradict the non-dual principle of Anthropic Divinity, they actually support it. For the Anthropically Divine principle insures that human beings will continually discover new and astonishing other cosmic possibilities. Continually and endlessly, never reaching the turtle at the bottom. Because in the act of discovering these possibilities, they will also thereby *create* them, endlessly. Even beyond string theory and multiple universes...what else? What next? Always something. Always deeper, more, and still more—the infinite erotic impulse to discover/create.

And consciousness will continue to generate these possibilities, if not through the medium of terrestrial human beings (who may not manage to survive themselves), then through the medium of Klingons, who knows? Doesn't really matter to consciousness.

The edifice of Darwinian evolution cannot remain untouched by this vision of the co-emergent participation of consciousness with phenomena. While the linear factualities of the evolution of species through natural selection are certainly true, they are true only on the most superficial level. Underlying this evolutionary process, and "breathing fire" into it (per Hawking's turn of phrase) is the same consciousness we've been talking about all along.

Although from the viewpoint of separateness, it certainly looks like evolution is following the laws of natural selection, and that this can explain everything from the feathers on a bird to the migration of whales; from the development of mitochondria that made complex, eukaryotic cells possible, to the convoluted, many-staged life cycle of the parasite that causes African sleeping sickness. Yet even the most educated person may harbor some doubt about such an explanation for all these fabulous natural displays, and it's not merely that they don't grasp the subtleties of Darwinian theory (although that's also often the case). No, it's because faced with the jaw-dropping improbability of the dramatic feats of mimicry performed by butterflies, they sense that there must be a flaw somewhere.

British astronomer Fred Hoyle once famously noted that there were approximately the same number of parts in a yeast cell as there were in a Boeing 747. We know that a jet airplane must be constructed according to a carefully planned blueprint, yet evolutionary science claims that a yeast cell, like all life forms, arose merely through chance mutation. So just imagine, said Hoyle, that a huge tornado blasted through a junkyard that just happened to contain all the bits and pieces of a Boeing 747. What is the chance that, once the dust had settled, a fully assembled 747, ready for take-off, would be found standing there?

Admittedly, this image is overstated, for the process of natural selection takes place not all-at-once, like a tornado, but rather piece-by-piece, mutation-by-mutation, over time. Still, the point may be instructive with regard to the role of random chance as the fundamental driver of evolution. Along similar lines, as the popular thought-experiment proposes, some researchers supposedly placed a bunch of typewriters in front of a group of monkeys to see what work of literary genius they would produce. But the unimaginative macaques typed nothing, favoring instead the use of the machines as toilets.

Although the story of this monkeyshine research must be apocryphal—who would have funded it?—the point may again be illustrative. How can an utterly random process explain the emergence of hummingbirds or platypuses? In response to this question, exoteric believers have come up with cockamamie alternative theories like intelligent design. But since that story also derives from a separative egoic viewpoint (an even less mature one, at that), it also fails to satisfy our doubts. For even if we haven't yet acknowledged it consciously, somehow we know that we are all connected in the expressive unfolding of the One (no)Thing, and that everything in that densely co-emergent web is evolving simultaneously with a beautifully entangled agreement throughout.

Which means that there *is* a supreme Intelligence that interpenetrates evolution, even if that intelligence is not outside somewhere or pulling any strings from an elevated distance. No, it's just that one of the inherent qualities of aware consciousness is intelligence.* And as that intelligence saturates all potential expression, it continually collapses the infinite possibilities of being into actual phenomenal creations, which in their beingness, reflect that conscious intelligence back to itself. In other words, evolution by natural selection may be relatively true, but it represents only a limited view of the Whole, whose activities are much more subtle, much more dark.

An ineffable intelligence underlies all evolutionary processes, but it does not dictate or control them. It merely permeates them in co-emergent embrace, photon by photon, not planning at all what's coming up next. A giraffe's neck? *Marvelous!* An octopus's eyeball? *Cool!* What an unexpected delight (thinks the Absolute). What a fantastic new way for Me to *know* Myself! "Consciousness is the greatest painter," said the Indian sage Nisargadatta Maharaj, "The whole world is a picture." And the greatest Appreciator of that picture is none other than...you guessed it.

So yes, from outside the system, natural selection can indeed account for the evolutionary spectacle. But we know by now that in reality there is no such thing as "outside." Where would that be? The genetic mutations that start the evolutionary cascade do indeed appear as random—but only when viewed by a distant observer who doesn't really exist as distant at all. From inside the system—which in reality is the only place there is—every mutation is both the cause and the effect of every other mutation everywhere else; and the entire enterprise is driven by an intelligence that lives within and *as* the totality. Every single evolutionary occurrence is happening...er, EverywhereAllAtOnce.

---

* Consciousness is not so much intelligent as it is Intelligence itself. Likewise: compassionateness, justness, beautifulness, humorousness, kindness and generousness.

Whatever the evolutionary appearance may be, however, it's not known until it actually appears in form. Until all possibilities collapse into an actuality. And then, all of creation can, as One, pronounce that form of appearance as *good*. Even as already, creation is evolving to the next form, always desiring, yearning, always reaching back toward its ultimate identity with that same One. But even that unfinished, non-culminating movement...is all Good.

XVI

PLATONIC HOOEY

There's something about mathematics that sets it apart from every other human enterprise. Its abstractions can be so pure, so immaculate, so rarefied, that they seem to belong to some Platonic ideal realm, separate and somehow beyond this one.

To listen to mathematicians describe the ecstasy of their obsession can make a grown man blush. In his memoir, Edward Frenkel quotes fellow mathematician Heinrich Hertz:

> One cannot escape the feeling that these mathematical formulas have an independent existence and an intelligence of their own, that they are wiser than we are, wiser even than their discoverers.

Frenkel himself does nothing to hide his own devotion:

> The fact that such objective and enduring knowledge exists (and moreover, belongs to all of us) is nothing short of a miracle. ...That these highly abstract notions [of mathematics] coalesce in such refined harmony is absolutely mind-boggling. It points to something rich and mysterious lurking beneath the surface, as if the curtain had been lifted and we caught glimpses of the reality that had been carefully hidden from us [in the Blindspot?].[56]

Yes, of all human endeavors, mathematics stands apart in its starkly abstract purity. When so many of the formulations of mathematics seem to reside perfectly in their own removed Platonic realm, it's a wonder that so many of them should also just happen to apply so perfectly to the natural world; and many physicists (including Einstein) have expressed this amazement. How just one single equation can govern everything from the propagation of light to the vibrations of a cello string, from the coiling of a spiral to the orbits of a planet—that is just bleeping cool. Philosopher Peter Russell has said of his youth, "If you had asked me then whether there was a God, I would have pointed to mathematics."[57]

But whether or not mathematics does indeed exist in some inconceivable Platonic realm (whatever that is), it's not worth debating here. Because whether it does or doesn't, as soon as it intersects with the human mind, mathematics must still obey the laws of all phenomenal existence. And then, it must submit to the restraints of duality, no differently than any other phenomenal manifestation. Which means that it too will always end up bumping against the same discovery/creation boundaries as any other field of human endeavor.

Even Frenkel, that consummate lover of mathematics, has said, "Every new piece of the [mathematical] puzzle gives us new insights, new tools to unravel the mystery. And each time, we are dazzled by the seemingly inexhaustible richness of the emerging picture."[58]

Yes. Because in the human mind the picture will *never* stop emerging. Even mathematics, that most exquisite discovery/creation of the human mind, can never penetrate to the source code of life, the universe, and everything. As Frenkel himself admits:

> Each new result [in mathematics] pushes back the veil covering the unknown, but what then becomes known doesn't simply encompass answers—it includes questions we didn't know how to ask, directions we didn't know we could explore.[59]

Endlessly. And so it goes, as long as we remain in the realm of the known, even if the boundaries of that realm get expanded many times over by our efforts. All we can ever hope to do with our minds is push back the borders of what physicist Marcello Gleiser calls the "island of knowledge." Since even the most exquisite of symbolic systems must remain incomplete,* we can never write the ultimate truth as a mathematical equation. "We need to have some cosmic humility in our [scientific] claims," says cosmologist Laurence Krauss, "even if such a thing is difficult for cosmologists."[60]

Whether we're talking about quadratic formulas or the clucking of chickens, however, it all comes down to the same thing: the Absolute unfurling into an ever-expanding manifest discovery/creation, while simultaneously re-furling back into itself, yet never becoming anything other than itself. And the only thing that matters is whether we want to take that exhilarating ride consciously—i.e., awake—or not.

And ditto, when it comes to psychology.

From the nondual perspective, the case of mathematics in particular is actually no different from the case of thought itself in general, whether that thought is about geometric theorems or your unresolved childhood issues. I'm making the leap here to make a point about how so many of us go about seeking our own personal source codes—which is to dive into an exploration of our psychological selves, our identified *me*'s. By means of any of the hundreds of psychological tools at our disposal, we can indeed uncover layer after layer of our psyches. And we get excited about each new discovery, certain that we're pushing back the veil, getting closer and closer to the core of those childhood issues—and the key to our essential security and happiness. After a while of this struggle, however—sometimes decades—we may find that the layers are endless, the discoveries inexhaustible, and we find ourselves

---

* See Gödel's infuriating "incompleteness theorem" (if you dare).

burdened with the same old neuroses with which we started, like some hapless Woody Allen character. For just as it is with mathematics, when it comes to the core of the *me*, there is simply no *there* there.

This is not to say there's not a place for psychology on anyone's personal thread towards truth. Nor that there's not a place for mathematics in humanity's search for reality. My task here is to simply point out the Blindspot: that mathematics, as beautifully pure as it can be, will never reach the Source. And that psychology, as useful as it can be along the way, will never reveal happiness. *Dixi.*

I will say this about mathematics, though. Of all the ways available to humans to even suspect that there *is* a kind of veil beyond which there *could be* a deeper dimension of reality, this discipline promises some of the most potent breadcrumbs. Yes, it's true that following any thread with sufficient sincerity can lead toward the veil, but still, the way of mathematics can offer a string with fewer kinks, fewer distractions, than most others—even notwithstanding my strained metaphors. But just as with any thread toward truth, you can either follow it forever, undoing knot after knot, dissolving boundary after boundary, just for the fun and delight the journey can provide. Or you can eventually—if what you want is truth and not just amusement—jump off the thread entirely (or more accurately, allow it to be dropped)...into the Unknown. You can always go back to it later, if you want. It will still be waiting for your adventures in controlled folly.

I've heard about a curious phenomenon showing up in scientific research these days: When certain generally accepted experimental studies from one era are replicated at a later time, the results can show a marked "decline effect." Which has some startling implications for real-world applications. Like: the "new generation" antipsychotic medications that seemed so effective in 1997, apparently losing much of their therapeutic power by 2007, when the same experiments are repeated. As observed in several different laboratory and clinical situations, it has looked as if the universe itself has been displaying a kind of inherent habituation to a mixed variety of experimental results, an unexplained evaporation of positive statistical significances. As if the universe gets used to any particular human intervention, forcing us back to the drawing board to come up with another one.

Naturally, this phenomenon is not widely reported, for it threatens to undermine the very foundations of the scientific method, that hallowed bulwark of Western thought. So naturally also, the scientists are scrambling to come up with all kinds of logical explanations for the decline effect, invoking flaws in experimental design or the biases lurking in the unconscious interference of the researchers. But none of these explanations fully explain the actual cases—which may be occurring much more frequently than they even know about (or want to know about). I can't even be certain that such cases are widespread beyond the medical/clinical domain.

But the very possibility of this effect tickles my fancy. The medication works, the medication doesn't work. Same controlled, double-blind input; different output, just separated by time. Hmmm. Back to square one—freshly, now.

Or possibly: Just one more example of how what we call the observable universe may be observing us just as much (and as creatively) as the other way around.

As lonely, hairless, upright primates we desperately clutch at anything solid and reliable out there that we can trust and rely upon, where we can finally take our stand; but every one of those would-be anchors inevitably slips through our grasping fingers like sand, again and again. When will we learn that there is *nothing* out there that is always true, always good, always trustable? Yet at the same time, does indeed exist, and is indeed findable—if we would only look in the right direction and then just open our hands and...*let go.*

XVII

WHAT'S LOVE GOT TO DO WITH IT?

O love that fires the sun,
Keep me burning.
—Bruce Cockburn

It should come as no surprise by now that when nondual realizers use the term "love," they are speaking about the same thing we refer to in common speech and usual experience—*and* is not at all the same. Although perhaps not as common as we would like to think, the kind of genuine love that can arise between ordinary men and women, men and men, women and women, mother and child, friend and friend…is nothing to be downplayed or undervalued. It's good stuff, indeed, and can mark the pinnacle of the lives of the relatively few people who can experience it.

The absolute perspective on love, however—which is love's own perspective of itself—is a love that's inherent to consciousness. That is, it's a love that's utterly independent of circumstance, whether such circumstances are filled with loving partners, friends, and gods, or lacking any of the above. It is not a product of meeting the right person or having a beautiful child or bonding with your dog. It is instead the very nature of your existence. It is the "root of the root of yourself," according to Rumi. It utterly pervades yourself and all of nature. To put an anthropomorphic spin to it, it is that which inspires the unmanifest Absolute to unfurl (or hurl?) itself into creative expression, to begin with. He's so in love that He just can't help himself from creating entire universes, and neither can She. In the end, love is that which breathes fire into suns and moons, all and everything, eternally. Not least *you*, dear reader.

Here are a few thumbnail hints regarding the nature of love, when he or she is undressed and stands naked before the bed of the heart:

- It is not an emotion, for it is not subject to change.
- Yet it is subject to *flow*; indeed, neverending flow is one of its most beguiling charms.
- What is called love as an emotion is the mere shadow of love as it is.
- Yet if emotional love is a shadow, it must be a shadow of *something*.
- That shadow is precious, as it is a vital clue to that which it is the shadow *of*.
- It is endlessly creative; it is that which propels desire into manifestation.
- It is new in every moment.
- If directed towards an object or person, that object or person will never appear the same from day to day, moment to moment.
- There is never any familiarity to it.
- It is experienced only when one has emptied him/herself *of* him/herself.
- Indeed, it is not really any kind of relationship at all, because it is the collapse of otherness, altogether.
- It gives rise to gratitude, invariably.

"Love is the name we give to consciousness when it awakens to its identity with all things," says Rupert Spira, when it recognizes itself *in* all things, *as* all things. "Love is the natural condition of consciousness when it is knowingly one with all things."[61] And when that happens, then those "ten thousand things" of the perceivable world no longer appear as outside appearances to some inside awareness, but rather in ecstatic "intimacy" with it, as Dogen said.* In other words, *in love.*

And although I enjoy watching rom-com movies as much as the next guy, if I imagine that there's anything *outside* myself—even romantic consummation or public adulation—that can give me *that* order of completion, *that* order of love, then I am sorely kidding myself.

This is not to say that even fully awakened beings are incapable of enjoying romantic or bonded human (or canine) relationships, one person to another apparent person (or dog). The teacher Lee Lozowick coined the term "enlightened duality" to describe the condition in which consciousness knowingly allows for the apparent separation between the subject and object, lover and beloved. As it says in the Zen proverb that you might recognize from the old Donovan song: "First there is a mountain [dualistic perception], then there is no mountain [nondual perception], then there is the mountain [enlightened dualistic perception]." As always, the nature of the actual situation depends upon where the alleged individuals are coming from. When you're seeing the mountain the third time, through awakened eyes, you're back where you started, but "seeing it for the first time." When applied to the phenomenon we call love, enlightened duality means that the separation implied by a lover in relationship with a beloved collapses before the clarity into truth with which the lovers are operating—the perspective that is not fooled by appearances, even while enjoying them to the hilt.

By the same token, even the imaginary conception of an external, personified God is entirely permissible from an enlightened dualistic viewpoint. One can savor an adoration-soaked relationship with such a god without worrying that you have broken any nondual laws.

Yet one more paradox to ponder.

---

* Thirteenth century Zen master.

XVIII

ALREADY DONE

> Religion is for people who are afraid of hell. Spirituality is for people who have been there.
>
> —Unknown

Let me tell you about my old friend Ray Price,* with whom I've (regrettably) long lost contact and who is no doubt no longer with us. Ray was a true original, a brilliant nobody from a hardcore Southern Baptist, daddy-abused background... who was somehow able to use the energy he derived from all that childhood trauma, plus a chronic pain condition that had driven him to the brink of suicide, to drive him to awakening, instead. In this scenario he illustrated for me a principle that both the teachers Byron Katie and Eckhart Tolle acted out later for so many thousands of other seekers: that often it is only suffering that can propel us out of our indifference to the essential nature of our existence. That only suffering can finally force us to ask the questions that really matter about who we are and what we're doing here. We are such a stubborn species.†

Ray used to say something that I'm just now getting, some 40 years later: "We're all just making it up as we go along," he would remark. And when he said that, he was not referring only to himself or me, personally, but rather the entire human race, as a collective conscious tide, and probably other species as well.

---

* No relation to the country singer, although he was a fan.

† I must correct myself by saying that suffering is *not* a prerequisite for awakening, just that it seems to be such an almost universal one amongst our stiff-necked kind.

It's so true, I've realized: We *are* all just making it up as we go along, step by stagger into the unknown. And the responsibility inherent in that is both profound and poignant. In our Oneness we are alone, for there is no other. And from this place we create what we discover, in the act of discovering it. There is no supernatural tailor directing this tailor-made enterprise. Nor need there be. For another wise thing that Ray said was this: "It's all already done."

On the nondual path, you are always forever at the beginning, no matter how far you may go. You're always at the beginning, yes, but as Eliot observed, "[You] know it for the first time," every time. Enlightenment does not signal the end of discovery, for the unfolding of discovery never ends, is infinite, and what you discover wasn't even there until you gave it your divinely co-emergent attention. Which may be another way of saying that you offer it your humble, wonderstruck devotion. As the Buddhists chant: "Always Being, Always Becoming"—both conditions occurring simultaneously in the Eternal Now: Already Done.

If I keep going on like this, I will have effectively talked myself into validating the existence of the Blindspot in our public discourses. To express this stuff in words can't help but make it sound far more exclusive and complicated than it actually is, when realized in experience. I'm just trying to help render the confluence between the understandings of nondual sages and the rest of us not quite so blinding. "The rest of us" includes the scientists and the social activists and the environmentalists and the believers and the nonbelievers and all the halfway intelligent seekers of any stripe, who just want to know the answers to two questions:

1) Is there really such a thing as absolute truth? And,

2) Can it ever be known?

As you know by now, the answer to the former question is Yes (although it's not a thing or a who). And the answer to the latter question is also Yes (although it cannot be done conceptually). And authentic guidance regarding both answers is abundantly available all around, especially these days, just beyond the periphery of our mainstream culture's vision.

Which recapitulates the two prongs of what I've been calling the Blindspot:

- The concealment of truth (which is nondual) by all the veils conjured by mind, both personal and collective, most dramatically expressed in the exoteric forms of religion and counter-religion today, plus acted out in almost every aspect of mainstream culture; and
- The obliviousness in mainstream global culture (and science) to the thriving parallel universe of esoteric spiritual teachers, schools, communities, and para-quantum scientists.

With a wider understanding of just the two answers stated above, as well as an appreciation of these two prongs, the Blindspot currently afflicting humanity might start to dissolve. However, as it is probably evident by now, the answers that are revealed, once the Blindspot has been penetrated and nondual truth is revealed, are not the kind of answers a person might desire. The puzzles are not so much solved as resolved; the questions are not so much answered as they are rendered moot. Which might not satisfy the mind, but given the looks of things today, would that be too great a sacrifice to make?

The looks of things today . . . indeed! Sure, it's true that doomsday predictions are nothing new in history. However, due to a combination of factors both technological and demographic, today we are confronted by an array of societal and planetary threats that are unprecedented.

The public fear generated by these threats has done nothing but sharpened the dualistic operating system by which most people live. If humanity started out using Duality OS v.1, today it lives under the sway of OS v.100. And one can see its results everywhere. It's hard to even imagine one single movement or proposition in the public arena that doesn't immediately produce its opposition. Vaccination-ers/anti-vaxxers; climate-change alarmists/climate-change poo-pooers; Holocaust survivors/Holocaust deniers; gun controllers/gun unfetterers; migrant welcomers/migrant blockers; public library fart-book protectors/public library fart-book burners; gas stove attackers/gas stove defenders; pro-choicers/pro-choicelessnessers; sane folks/flat earthers… Anywhere you see an army of protesters on the news, you can see the army of anti-protesters screaming their insults across the flimsy guardrail separating them. For whatever it may be worth in the transcendent big picture, things don't look good on this particular planet.

My favorite writer, Romain Gary, who barely survived his service in the French Resistance during World War Two, became so despondent by what he called the unremitting "stupidity of mankind" that he committed suicide in 1980 at the age of 66. Although I am not recommending that anyone follow his example, I have certainly come to understand where he was coming from. I can just imagine what he would think today, were he able to look around!

What Gary called "stupidity," the Buddhists call "ignorance," in the nonjudgmental sense that it's simply a matter of people's ignoring the truth of their own actual nature. Another way of saying Blindspot. The teacher Adyashanti has delivered some withering remarks about the more earthbound dangers carried by the Blindspot, if it remains such. "The world's problems," he says,

> are by and large human problems—the unavoidable consequences of egoic sleepwalking. If we care to look, all the signs are present to suggest that we are not only

> sleepwalking, but at times borderline insane as well. We try very hard not to notice, because we don't want to see how asleep we are, how desolate our condition really is. So, we blindly carry on.

Again: the not-seeing. Not recognizing what is blazingly spread out before us.

Adyashanti goes on:

> We have sailed the ship of delusion about as far as she can carry us. We have run her ashore and now find ourselves shipwrecked on an increasingly desolate land. … *Wake up or perish* is the spiritual call of our times.

But of course, like the true sage he is, Adyashanti concludes his rant with the higher, even truer view: *"And yet all is eternally well, and more well than can be imagined."*[62]

We're back to the image of the Divine Mother from Chapter One—she who weeps for us with eyes that remain dry. Like Adyashanti, she knows that all is eternally well. Yet she also knows that Earth might well be doomed, along with all your children and grandchildren and countless nonhuman animals. But which is true? Are we doomed or not? Is Her heartbreak genuine or not? Well, both, of course…or maybe neither. Don't even try to figure it out.

The various ways available to "not figuring it out" go well beyond the scope of this book—and I took pains to avoid recommending specific teachers or teachings. But such ways are largely mysterious. Sure, someone could list a number of guidelines that might alert the seeker to the well-known traps and deceptions that anyone might encounter along the path, but fundamentally the journey is generated from something alive within each person. The truth—which is not other than every person's own true nature—possesses an inherent yearning to recognize and honor itself; and the thread towards that truth is unique to each one. If the seeker is ruthlessly honest enough with him- or herself, that truth will out. You can trust *that*, no matter what. There is a time-tested science of a different sort to this esoteric brand of looking, one in which the seeker's laboratory is his very own self, and where no results are acceptable until born out empirically. And where, as in any true science, such results are falsifiable, when tested in living experience.

As an example: Someone once asked me what I thought about celibacy. The doctrine of her path insisted that everyone needed to remain celibate until marriage. *Everyone*, period.

I was appalled. Sure, for some people celibacy might be a useful practice at certain times, during certain phases. But like all purported spiritual practices, the applications must be suited to the individual, tailored precisely to each person's unique process along the way. And it's up to the individual him/herself to decide whether the experiment was fruitful or not. As Sting said, "They go crazy in congregations; they only get better one by one."

Whether or not they have a guru or guide, most people end up following a zig-zag course. But in reality there's no wasted time, no wasted effort. Even should you get hijacked by some manner of exoteric groupthink, this will only tend to slow down your arrival to where all roads lead—the Inevitable.

Possessing an active mind myself, I realize that for every assertion made in this book, dozens of questions and objections will be made. One of the most profound (and beautiful) paradoxes inherent in non-dual teachings could be stated as follows: Nonduality is that which couldn't be simpler. And...the pie that expresses this simplicity can be sliced in an inexhaustible variety of portions and spiced with a myriad of seemingly incongruent condiments.

I therefore hope the reader will forgive me if I leave this particular expression with loose or even contradictory threads, for that is just the nature of the game. Whether or not anybody decides to engage the science described here, though, *it's all already done*—whatever the "it" may be. As The Walrus sang, "Nothing to get hung about."

For in the final freedom, there's no such thing, really, as exoteric religion or esoteric spirituality. There is neither duality nor nonduality, relative nor absolute, asleep nor awake, low nor high. Once your vision has clarified, you can see that it's all a bunch of hooey, even the most sublime of it. There's no such thing as even spirituality itself. I mean, what could possibly be the *opposite* of that? Which is like asking what is the opposite of God?*

All such separative words are merely linguistic tricks meant to drive the mind out of its linguistic tricks. Things are no more spiritual than they are mundane (or even profane), and things are no more mundane than they are spiritual. The distinctions are fine to play with in the world of appearances, but guaranteed to cause trouble if you cling to them. The finger pointing at the moon is not the moon. Nor is the taxidermied moose a moose (whatever that means).

After all, from God's own perspective he is neither limited or unlimited, finite or infinite, for to be one thing or the other, there would need to be something other than himself for him to compare himself *to*. She neither gets to be born nor to die, for to experience one thing or the other, there would need to be some kind of existence other than hers to compare her own existence *to*. And there ain't.

Sure, at times it may be appropriate to function in the domain of duality and sometimes it's appropriate to function in the domain of the

---

* And if you answered Satan, you might hear the sound of a loud, annoying buzzer.

nondual; and one's perception of reality will appear in congruence with either way. Yet at the same time, any attempt to locate the boundary between the relative and the absolute, between form and the formless, is not possible, because they are just like "two arrows meeting in mid-air," as the *Sandokai* of Zen asserts. They explode/implode into nothingness.

Or, to take it even one step further (stay with me here): Since there is only ever One (no)Thing happening at any moment, and it is neither the subject *to* anything nor the object *of* anything (or is both subject and object in eternal self-reflexive embrace)...*and* that "at any moment" is always not other than the eternal Now...then:

Nothing actually ever happened.

The light of pure knowing (consciousness/awareness) has never abandoned itself. There was never any separation to begin with; the One has never stopped being itself. The Alpha was never not always the Omega, even as time's play has unspooled between them. All that is or was or ever will be—just an unspooling of something out of nothing, while remaining nothing. The whole damn kit and caboodle—forgetting and remembering; Big Bang and multiverses: *Poof.* Never happened at all.

Although I'm not sure the IRS would agree.

I'll leave you with an ancient Upanishadic chant, which sums it all up, um...wholo-graphically.

> That is Whole, this also is Whole,
> This Whole came from that Whole.
> Though this Whole came from that Whole,
> That Whole remains forever Whole.

Some translations use the word "Perfect" in place of "Whole." The choice is yours to make…even if it isn't.

CITATIONS

1. Whitman, Walt. *Song of Myself*, 1855.
2. Barrett, Justin. *Born Believers: The Science of Children's Religious Belief.* New York: Atria Books, 2012.
3. Laing, R.D. source unknown.
4. Blanton, Brad. *Radical Honesty: How to Transform Your Life by Telling the Truth*. Sparrowhawk Publications, 2005. Kindle loc. 2606.
5. R.D. Laing. source unknown.
6. Blanton. op. cit., loc. 838.
7. McKenna, Jed. *Spiritual Enlightenment, The Damnedest Thing*. Wisefool Press, 2011.
8. Spira, Rupert. *The Transparency of Things: Contemplating the Nature of Experience.* Salisbury, UK: Non-Duality Press, 2008, p. 38.
9. Spira, Rupert. source unknown.
10. Kiloby, Scott. *Reflections of the One Life*. Salisbury, UK: Non-Duality Press, 2014, p. 74.
11. Carse, David. *Perfect Brilliant Stillness*. Paragaté Publishing, 2017, loc. 4509.
12. Spira, Rupert. *The Transparency of Things*. op. cit.
13. Wallis, Christopher D. *The Recognition Sutras: Illuminating a 1000-Year-Old Spiritual Masterpiece.* Boulder, Colorado: Mattamayura Press, 2017, p. 151.
14. Lott, Joey. *The Best Thing That Never Happened.* Salisbury, UK: Non-Duality Press, 2014, p. 78.
15. Russell, Peter. *From Science to God: A Physicist's Journey into the Mystery of Consciousness*. Novato, California: New World Library, 2004, p. 81.
16. Lucille, Francis and Pépin, Catherine. *Brain, Mind, Cosmos: The Nature of Our Existence and the Universe.* Sages & Scientists Series, Deepak Chopra, Editor, Part 1, 2014, loc. 8323.
17. Eliot, T.S. *Four Quartets*, 1943.
18. McKenna, Jed. op. cit.
19. Castaneda, Carlos. *Journey To Ixtlan: The Lessons of Don Juan*. New York: Washington Square Press, 1991.
20. Lozowick, Lee. *Just This 365: Wisdom and Wit from the Teachings of Lee Lozowick*. Chino Valley, Arizona: Hohm Press, 2017, p. 18.

21. Russell, Peter. op. cit., p. 128.
22. Lozowick, Lee. op. cit., p. 15.
23. Tillich, Paul. *Dynamics of Faith*. San Francisco: Harper One, 2009.
24. De Zengotita, Thomas. *Mediated: How the Media Shapes Your World and the Way You Live in It*. London: Bloomsbury Publishing, 2006, p. 9.
25. Turner, Jack. *The Abstract Wild*. Tucson: The University of Arizona Press, 1996, p. 17.
26. Benazzo, Zaya and Maurizio, Eds. *On the Mystery of Being: Contemporary Insights on the Convergence of Science and Spirituality*. Oakland, California: Reveal Press (New Harbinger), 2019, p. xii.
27. James, William. *The Varieties of Religious Experience: A Study in Human Nature*, 1902.
28. Watts, Alan. *The Book: On the Taboo Against Knowing Who You Are*. New York: Vintage Books, 2011.
29. Leary, Timothy; Metzner, Ralph; Alpert, Richard. *The Psychedelic Experience: A Manual Based on the Tibetan Book of the Dead*. Secaucus, NJ: Citadel Press, 1964.
30. Clayton, Philip from Davies and Gregerson, Eds. *Information and the Nature of Reality from Physics to Metaphysics*. Cambridge: Cambridge University Press, 2014, p. 40.
31. Rosenblum, Bruce and Kuttner, Fred. *The Quantum Enigma: Physics Encounters Consciousness*. Oxford: Oxford University Press, 2011, p. 265.
32. Davies, Paul and Gregerson, Niels Henrik, Eds. *Information and the Nature of Reality: From Physics to Metaphysics*. Cambridge: Cambridge University Press, 2010, p. 68.
33. Chopra, Deepak, Ed. *Brain, Mind, Cosmos*. op. cit., loc. 8486.
34. Chopra, Deepak, Ed. Ibid., loc. 9435.
35. Chopra, Deepak, Ed. Ibid., loc. 2852.
36. Chopra, Deepak, Ed. Ibid., loc. 9663.
37. Spira, Rupert. op. cit., p. 207.
38. Gleiser, Marcelo. *The Island of Knowledge: The Limits of Science and the Search for Meaning*. Philadelphia: Basic Books, 2014, p. 174.
39. Rosenblum, Bruce and Kuttner, Fred. op. cit., p. 189.
40. Ibid., p. 101.
41. Spira, Rupert. op. cit.
42. Andrews, Sperry. source unknown.
43. Wallis, Christopher D. op. cit., p. 80.

44. Andrews, Sperry. source unknown.
45. Gould, Stephen Jay. *Rocks of Ages: Science and Religion in the Fullness of Life*. New York: Ballantine Books, 2011.
46. Krauss, Laurence. *A Universe from Nothing: Why There Is Something Rather Than Nothing*. Atria Books, 2012. p. 34.
47. Aczel, Amir D. *Why Science Does Not Disprove God*. New York: William Morrow, 2014, p. 4
48. Krauss, Laurence. op. cit., p. 117.
49. Krauss, Laurence. Ibid. p. 125.
50. Rosemblum and Kuttner. op. cit., p. 268.
51. Gleiser, Marcelo. op. cit., p. 197.
52. Rosenblum and Kuttner. op. cit., p. 219.
53. Gleiser, Marcelo. op. cit., p. 223.
54. Chopra, Deepak, Ed. op. cit., loc. 3152
55. Liquorman, Wayne. *Acceptance of What Is*. Advaita Press, 2000, p. 47.
56. Frenkel, Edward. *Love and Math*. New York: Basic Books, 2013, p. 91.
57. Russell, Peter. op. cit., p. 5.
58. Frenkel, Edward. op. cit., p. 184.
59. Frenkel, Edward. Ibid. p. 182.
60. Krauss, Laurence. op. cit., p. 118.
61. Spira, Rupert. op. cit.
62. Adyashanti. *The Way of Liberation: A Practical Guide of Spiritual Enlightenment*. Campbell, California: Open Gate Sangha, p. xiii.

ABOUT THE AUTHOR

Moss Campion. While growing up on the mist-shrouded coast of Maine, Moss Campion would eagerly await the arrival of Halloween all year long, already demonstrating his strong interest in the numinous side of life. Even as he later worked in fields as varied as music, skiing and journalism, he persisted in his spiritual pursuits, studying with a number of esteemed teachers and mentors. In addition, his many years of employment as a registered nurse gave him wide exposure to the grittier aspects of life, which deeply informed his mystical understandings.

Campion also holds a master's degree in journalism and has numerous credits in specialized magazines and corporate publications; and his biography of the Bavarian sage Lothar Weichert was published in Germany in 2006. He has received awards and fellowships from University of Michigan, University of Denver, University of Colorado, and the Ucross Foundation.

Contact information: aurorapmoss@gmail.com

ABOUT HOHM PRESS

Hohm Press is committed to publishing books that provide readers with alternatives to the materialistic values of the current culture, and promote self-awareness, the recognition of interdependence, and compassion. Our subject areas include parenting, transpersonal psychology, religious studies, women's studies, the arts and poetry.

Contact Information: Hohm Press, PO Box 4410, Chino Valley, Arizona, 86323, USA; 800-381-2700, or 928-636-3331; email: publisher@hohmpress.com

Visit our website at www.hohmpress.com